S

Antisemitism, Racism and the Limits of Diversity

Strange Hate:

Antisemitism, Racism and the Limits of Diversity

Keith Kahn-Harris

Published by Repeater Books
An imprint of Watkins Media Ltd

Unit 11Shepperton House
89-93 Shepperton Road
London
N1 3DF
United Kingdom
www.repeaterbooks.com
A Repeater Books paperback original 2019
1

Distributed in the United States by Random House, Inc., New York.

Cover design: Johnny Bull
Typography and typesetting: Frederik Jehle
Typefaces: Meriden LT Std, Crete Round

ISBN: 9781912248438
Ebook ISBN: 9781912248445

Printed and bound in the United Kingdom by TJ International Ltd

CONTENTS

PREFACE

Humans, Politics and Identities

This is an infuriating book, about an infuriating phenomenon produced by the most infuriating beings there are — human beings.

I talk a lot about humans in this book. I am one of course, so I feel I can speak with some authority. My vision for humanity is pretty simple: Broadly speaking, I would prefer it if my fellow humans and I would avoid killing, torturing, enslaving and raping each other at the very least. Even better would be if we could find a way to ensure that we can live without persecution, structural disadvantage and abuse.

So far so bland. But I'm under no illusions about what human beings are actually like. Broadly speaking, I'm not a big fan of our species in general and of myself in particular. There are parts of myself and things that I have done that disgust me. I am full of rage and desire. Within me is a constant struggle between what Jewish theology calls the *yetzer ha-tov* and the *yetzer ha-ra* — the good inclination and the bad inclination. Whether one balances the other out is for others to judge; I am certainly in no position to make that tally myself.

In wanting us to get along with each other, I am not calling for some kind of holy communion of our mutual *yetzer tovim*. If there is to be any chance to remake a world in which we can let go of our human tendency to abuse, it has to account for our dark, unlikeable inclinations. That means acknowledging that we will not only dislike others, we will hate them too. This is, in my view, ineradicable – a permanent fact. Somehow, we have to find a way to get along with people we hate.

I doubt that, outside of eschatological theology, many people think that hate can be abolished. What is much more common though, is the hope that we may be able to abolish hatred of entire categories of people and restrict our hatred to individuals as individuals. Many us yearn to eradicate hatred of the entire membership of religious, ethnic, national, sexual and other groups. The challenge we face is coming to terms with *identity*, the human tendency to attach themselves or others to something bigger than themselves, and the frequent tendency of humans to be suspicious of or opposed to those holding other identities. Eradicating identity-based hate requires, in some views, reconciliation, dialogue and empathy between holders of different identities. Alternatively, or perhaps simultaneously, eradicating identity-based hate may mean uncompromising opposition to the haters, marginalising them, even fighting them. Others would argue that it is the identities that are the problem and that if we relate to individuals as individuals, we will then begin to see them as humans with whom we can coexist.

As a sociologist, I see group identities as social facts. I am agnostic as to whether they are essential to us as humans, but I find it very hard to envisage a time when we will be entirely free of them, whether we would wish that or not. We are bound into group identities even if we refuse them, even when we assert our utter individual uniqueness. It is certainly possible and desirable to treat identity as more open, fluid and syncretic — non-*essentialist* — both intellectually and as a practice. Yet while we may be able to control how and whether we personally identify with a particular group, we can rarely control whether other people will identify us with it. And whilst a world in which no one identifies as anything other than themselves seems to be out of reach, even if we *could* reach it this would endanger the possibilities for nurturance and community between those who see each other as alike.

I am also pessimistic as to whether we can abolish hatred of other groups, although we can certainly go much further along the road towards doing so than we have so far. The reason for this is that there is one facet of identity that presents the greatest impediment to getting along and is often (although definitely not always) part of the identity package. That facet of identity is "the political" — viewpoints, visions for the future, projects and ideologies. Members of religions, ethnic groups and nations often have a tendency not just to share a particular kind of politics *but also to see it as an inextricable part of their identity*. That doesn't mean that all members of a group share the same politics, but they may share the conviction that their politics is an integral feature of the identity they carry. For example, both Zionist and anti-Zionist Jews may see their stance on Zionism as rooted in Jewish history, tradition and ideals.

This presents a massive problem. Ideally, the political is always contestable; indeed its contestability is what should define it. Yet to contest some forms of politics inevitably means contesting group identities. And however much we might wish to get along with bearers of diverse identities, it surely asks too much that we abjure any kind of criticism of the politics that they bring with them.

A significant proportion of this book discusses one example of the consequences of not recognising the inextricable linkage between politics and identity. Many but not all Jews today are Zionists in some shape or form. Zionism is a political ideology. When Zionism and the legitimacy of the state of Israel are attacked, many Jews experience this as antisemitism.[1] Those doing the attacking usually find this incomprehensible at the very least. For the most part they do not see themselves as attacking Jews — only their politics — indeed, they may see themselves as defenders of Jews against hatred.

As I will argue, controversies over Jews, Israel, Zionism and antisemitism raise much broader questions about anti-racism and the politics of diversity. The refusal to acknowledge or accept the fact that identities are often political identities has contributed to a growing "selectivity" in choosing which groups to defend or damn.

The "solution" (if it can be called that) that I offer, will not be one of reconciliation. Rather, I will suggest an anti-racist politics predicated on acknowledging the hatefulness of others. I will stare into the abyss and try and formulate a way of living with diversity that accepts that a slice of that diversity will be hateful to even the most convinced anti-racist. I will also try and reconstruct a form of politics that is appropriate to the challenge diversity poses.

Some might accuse me of excessive pessimism and of underestimating the human capacity to maintain relationships with others across the widest divides, political or otherwise. I accept the good faith of those who make this criticism. While I am indeed highly sceptical of whether the knot of politics and group identities can ever be unpicked, if there is any chance that it can happen, it will require at the very least a recognition that they exist for now. If humans are ever to break free of seeing their politics as part of their group identities, then it will have to come about through a free choice, rather than compulsion.

What I call in this book "selective anti/racism" has emerged as a response to the knot of politics and group identity. The fact of inconvenient political identities has made it too difficult for anti-racists to be universally anti-racist. Conversely, racists have discovered that they could leaven their racism, and even indemnify themselves against accusations of racism, through reaching out to politically convenient others.

As I will argue, selective anti/racism is a growing and urgent problem, and "selective anti/semitism" is its cutting edge. The phenomenon is endangering the possibility of living together peacefully in diverse societies. There are two ways to fight it. One would be the universal disentanglement of politics and identity, which is almost certainly unachievable under current conditions, assuming that it is desirable in the first place. The other is to rethink what anti-racism and diversity mean; this is the course I follow in this book.

INTRODUCTION

Harmony Corruption

On a sunny Sunday in June, the local park near my house in North London looks like a vision of multicultural harmony.

Queuing up for the ice cream van manned by a friendly Cypriot are middle-class white families drawn from the spacious homes that abut the park. On the boating lake, large, modestly-dressed Haredi Jewish families pack into pedalos and set off on the water. On the grass, Bangladeshi Muslim groups enjoy elaborate picnics prepared by headscarf-wearing women. A young Afro-Caribbean man spray-paints the graffiti wall, watched by a multi-ethnic group of skateboarders. A Nigerian-born couple and their kids take a post-church stroll in their best clothes. Turkish-speaking youths bounce a football. Polish waitresses serve coffee in the cafe.

It wouldn't take much, though, for this vision of multicultural harmony to collapse.

The friendly Cypriot ice cream man spends every winter in his native village — what dark secrets might it hold from the conflict that tore the island apart? Those white middle-class families from my own impeccably liberal neighbourhood — are they the ones who have been posting paranoia on Facebook about moped-riding muggers from the largely black neighbourhood next to ours? Those strictly orthodox Jewish families — are they threatening family members who want to leave the community? What do the Bangladeshi families feel about Islamist extremism? Is the Afro-Caribbean graffiti artist one of the local gang members slaughtering rivals on the streets? Do the Nigerian couple share the homophobia endemic to African Christianity? Did the Turkish footballers post the pro-Erdoğan flyers that I saw in a nearby neighbourhood? Do the Polish waitresses support their country's crackdown on an independent judiciary?

And what about me? What would happen if my confreres in cosmopolitanism knew that I was Jewish? Would they see me as a supporter of the Zionist entity? A white colonial oppressor? Or would they see me as someone on the heroic frontline against the Muslim hordes? Some might think of me as not a proper Jew because, whilst I have a long beard, I don't wear a black coat in summer and eight modestly-clad children do not trail after me. Perhaps I am one of those Jews who are subverting socialism through fake claims of antisemitism! Or the reverse: maybe I am one of those self-hating Jews who provide cover for the antisemites in the Labour Party!

They don't know me. And I don't know anything about the other visitors to the park. We are ignorant of each other, save the limited signals that dress codes, faces and speech provide. That ignorance undergirds the multicultural bliss. But for how much longer will this lack of knowledge persist? The strains are already starting to show as the online world reveals to us the incommensurate agendas that we (usually) avoid revealing in public spaces.

What we are now being forced to confront is an aspect of multicultural diversity that is neither enriching, colourful nor vital. We are faced with the dread that opens up once you engage with the close, inescapable presence of others whose politics cannot be reconciled with your own. A hidden fear of this abyss lurks amidst the celebratory rhetoric about diversity. The convivial co-existence that seems so effortless in a North London park faces collapse into paranoia.

***

Are you still with me? So far, it probably looks like I've written one of *those* books, written by supposedly liberal authors, that tell us that multiculturalism has "failed", that unbridled diversity can only ever lead to turmoil, that immigration is a destabilising force. Maybe you expect the following pages to contain an abundance of head-shaking sighs that "well it was a noble idea but it was never going to work". Perhaps you imagine I will argue that it is better to integrate difference into a renewed whole, to repair the wounds that the post-war multiculturalist experiment has caused.

No, this is not one of those books. I will not be arguing that we need to retreat from promoting diversity and multiculturalism; I will not be advocating a renewed focus on integration. Nor will this book offer a tirade against immigration. Not only do I believe that immigration policies are too restrictive in most Western democracies, I would argue that we can and should prepare to accept immigrants on an unprecedented scale in the next few decades. In a world ravaged by climate change, accepting millions of refugees will be an ethical imperative, particularly for those countries whose carbon lust initiated the crisis in the first place. It may well be that a world without borders, or at least, less rigidly-policed borders, is an imperative in the anthropocene. That means we must cultivate a much more resilient attitude to immigration, regardless of what its costs might or might not be.

I see myself as an anti-racist. I am informed by the left anti-racist tradition in post-war politics, a tradition that has deconstructed the racist and colonial underpinnings of Western culture and argued for a cosmopolitan future in a globalised world. What I am arguing though is that this tradition has never fully grasped the sheer difficulty of the challenge of building diverse societies. A bloodless version of the rhetoric (if not necessarily the practice) of anti-racism has become normative in recent decades in many democratic societies. This apparent consensus has proved a barrier, rather than a spur, to addressing difficult questions of how we live alongside people whose views, identities and practices we find bewildering, unpleasant and hateful. We have avoided asking whether we can really live alongside those people that every fibre of our being tells us to despise.

How to live together is not a new question; it has been discussed at least as long as humans first started living together in cities. The burghers of the Greek polis grappled with how one could take the diverse raw material of human society and build a collective entity bigger than the individual without crushing individuality. What is new (or at least greatly accelerated) is the complexity of society, the degree of interconnection between its members and the ambition with which we aspire to reconcile multiple collective identities within one greater identity. It has become normative to at least pay lip service to the idea that we can be, simultaneously, unique individuals, bearers of religious, ethnic or other kinds of collective identities, and citizens of countries, regions, cities and the world. And on top of that, we are compelled to do so without seeking to physically wipe out or persecute others who share the same space as us but have antithetical politics.

It's a big ask.

While this difficulty is not a reason to refuse the challenge, we should not shirk from accepting the fact of its arduousness. In fact, a tacit recognition of this has long been implicit in the subtle and not-so-subtle partiality with which even the most passionate anti-racists have embraced diversity. For most of us, there has usually been a bit of ourselves that never really reconciled ourselves to the presence of portions of the ethnicities, religions and peoples that infused the Western world in the age of globalisation. We chose to focus on the people we could relate to, the ones we could defend — or at least on our fantasies of what these people really were. We sought out the minorities within minorities, the parts of these communities that we were politically comfortable with. We *selected*.

Racists also learned the same trick. Most of them abandoned the desire to rid the world of or subjugate absolutely everyone not like themselves. Instead, they selected those minorities, or minorities within minorities, who could not be redeemed, who could never be good people living alongside themselves, and focused on restricting, abusing or expelling them. They learned to divide and rule, to play favourites.

What I call selective anti-racism and selective racism have now become the dominant racisms and anti-racisms of our times. Not only do they mirror each other, they are frequently the corollary of the other. To select one minority, or minority within a minority, to defend against racism, is to abandon the rest to their dismal fate, or even to collude in it. In order to draw attention to the intimate relationship between selective anti-racism and selective racism, I offer in this book the neologism "selective anti/racism".

Selective anti/racism might have been kept under control, simply an unpleasant tendency rather than the dominant way of relating to minorities, were it not for the online revolution that has occurred in the last couple of decades. The explosion of online opinion, the provision of platforms to even the tiniest fringe group, has confronted us with the sheer breadth and depth of diversity as never before. We know more about the people we are living alongside, and often we don't like what we see.

More than any other minority, it has been Jews like me who have precipitated the development of selective anti/racism. Of course it has! We Jews have a way of forcing the issue. We were the ones who provided *the* test case in the development of enlightened modernity, the boundaries of what kind of diversity could be possible in the liberal nation state. We were the ones who experienced the genocide that haunts the modern imagination. We were the ones who built the Israeli state that consumes the world's attention.

And we cannot shut up. We proclaim our Jewishness to the world. We disagree with each other in public and reveal to everyone else that we are internally diverse, fractious and awkward. So profound is our disagreement, we cannot even agree what the form of racism that targets us — antisemitism — consists of.

In recent years, this has been our greatest gift to the world. We have provided a way of circumventing the challenge of diversity, by promiscuously offering an indemnity against seeing yourself as antisemitic. If one set of Jews don't appeal, you can reject them, safe in the knowledge that some of us will reassure you that you are not an antisemite. You can select the Jews you like and the antisemitism that you wish to oppose, and we will support you in this endeavour. Where Jews go, others follow. The emergence of selective anti/semitism paved the way for other selective anti/racisms. Muslims are starting to scramble to be the good Muslims, to give non-Muslims the gift of an Islamophobia they can live with. Perhaps this process is less-developed with some groups — the Roma remain gloriously unclubbable — but it cannot be long before they, too, catch up.

So pernicious has selective anti/racism become that it is becoming a major impediment to nurturing the tools we need to face the challenges that diversity presents. If we are not careful, we will reach the situation where no one will be racist anymore, and everyone will be a racist.

This process is a bewildering one. Racism is often associated with hate. The hatred produced by selective anti/racism is strange indeed. It is a form of hatred that insists that it is otherwise. It is hate produced within an economy of denial and accusation that confuses everyone involved to the point of exhaustion. Our propensity for racism has become unrecognisable to ourselves.

***

In what follows, I will try and make the strange hate of selective anti/racism recognisable, through a sustained discussion of what I call "the antisemitism controversy". By this I mean the cycle of accusations and denials of antisemitism that have permeated left-wing politics for years and have more recently spread to the right. While the antisemitism controversy is worthy of attention in and of itself, its implications go to the heart of the challenges of living with diversity. In response, I will present an argument for embracing diversity, but a diversity without illusions. The vision I will offer will be one in which diverse societies manage the tensions that arise within them with what I call "sullen solidarity" and "minimal civility". Mine will be a doleful vision of self-restraint and careful interaction. That I have the temerity to present this as somehow radical says something of how far we have fallen and how great the challenge is.

As the reader will have noticed already, I am fond of addressing the "we". Who is this "us"? At times it includes my fellow Jews; at others it is my fellows on the political left; sometimes I speak to those of us who live in "Western" societies or even humanity more generally. I do not speak from one standpoint. I am deeply involved in Jewish communal life in Britain, both professionally and as a Jew in the pew. I am ambivalent about some aspects of my Jewish community; my views on Israel and Zionism are more critical than most, although I do not define myself as anti-Zionist and cannot deny the depth of my (often uneasy) relationship to Israel. I define myself as left-wing, my views predicated on a refusal of the "capitalist realism" that renders the world as it is as the only world that could be.[1] Yet I don't consider the world after the capitalocene to necessarily be a utopia; there are engrained human pathologies that will persist beyond capitalism. I don't always find it easy to find a place for myself within some left-wing movements.

We're all awkward to define aren't we? Defining individuals as bearers of an identity can be a violent imposition. Identities and definitions can also be willingly self-imposed. Somehow, to speak of humans as anything other than atomised individuals, we must pick a path between these two poles. The best I can do here is to cultivate an ambiguity around the terms I use. When I speak of "humans", "Jews", "the left" or "the right" without other qualifications, I am trying to maintain the possibility that the reader might find a way to see themselves in what I write. I want to include as many of us as possible in the discussion of the strange hate of selective anti/semitism and selective anti/racism because I believe that many if not most of us can fall into it. This was an uncomfortable book to write as I was talking at times about myself — and I hope it will be equally uncomfortable to read as I might well be talking about you.

While there is no part of the political spectrum that is free of selective anti/racism, in this book I am particularly concerned with the left. This is partially because I define myself as of the left and so this is an issue in which I have a strong personal stake. But more importantly, selective anti-racism on the left *should* attract more attention than that of the right for the simple reason that anti-racism has become central to the self-definition of left-wing politics. As with anything else in life, if you set a high standard, you should expect closer scrutiny.

Speaking very broadly, the difference between left and right may be that, for selective anti/racists on the right it is the anti-racism that provides the jarring exception, and on the left it is the racism that does not fit the general picture. Jews and anti/semitism are the source of both exceptions: activists on the right sometimes defend Jews and no other minority, activists on the left sometimes attack Jews and no other minority.

Even if racism is a much more persistent problem on the right of the political spectrum, addressing the selectivity and blind spots on the left is still an urgent problem. If those at the vanguard of anti-racism can fall prey to selectivity, what hope is there for the rest? A reckoning with selective anti/racism on the left can therefore pave the way for a broader reckoning with the blind spots in dealing with diversity.

For that reason, sections of this book are tacitly addressed to those on the left who have been accused of antisemitism. I do this not to reinforce the accusations, but to attempt to persuade that there is another way: it *is* possible to retain a commitment to Palestinian liberation, to criticise Israel, without becoming embroiled in controversies over antisemitism. That said, there is no doubting the difficulty of doing so. It requires nothing less than rethinking what anti-racism means.

So this book is preoccupied with questions over antisemitism on the left, but this is not its beginning and end. The first few chapters concentrate on antisemitism before the book broadens out to consider what the controversy over antisemitism today tells us about diversity and anti-racism. This is not a parochial issue, even when it has parochial effects.

***

Well, okay, I will concede that maybe this book will seem a *bit* parochial in places. I can't deny that the initial motivating force behind this book was my own desire to understand and respond to the ongoing controversy over antisemitism in the UK Labour Party. Since Jeremy Corbyn was elected Labour leader in September 2015, I have been immersed in this fierce conflict. While the controversy has received a fair amount of publicity worldwide, it is likely that only people in the UK will have followed all its twists and turns. In fact, even in the UK there is a gap between those who are intensely invested in the issue — Jews, pro-Palestinian campaigners, Labour Party activists — and everyone else.

I don't assume in this book that every reader will be as preoccupied with this particular controversy as I am. But it remains a vitally important case study for illuminating the troubling questions I raise in this book. Antisemitism on the left and on other parts of the political spectrum has, in the last few years, been revived as a political issue in many countries. In the US, for example, controversies about the exclusion of Zionists from progressive movements have unfolded in a very similar way to those regarding the place of Zionists in Corbyn's Labour Party.

The significance of the British case study is partially that it is the leader of the main opposition party — one that may even be in power by the time this book is published — who has been accused of left antisemitism. Further, the party he leads has a long and deep history of Jewish involvement, both Zionist and anti-Zionist. The intractable controversy over antisemitism in the party has not been a side issue, of concern only to Jews, but a headline issue. While you can find some of these features in other controversies in other countries, the UK case brings them together in a uniquely acute and visible way.

The British case does not supply the beginning and end of understanding antisemitism, racism and the politics of diversity. At the very least though, it would be hard to understand what they mean today without engaging with what has happened within the British Labour Party. Those who read the book may be immersed in other toxic controversies in other parts of the world, including some (such as the controversy over antisemitism that has torn apart the Women's March in the US) that are also referred to in this book. Perhaps understanding what has happened in Britain might be a place to begin to understand the situation elsewhere. Or maybe we in the UK stand as a warning over how difficult things can get if the questions I raise remain unaddressed.

In any case, the examples discussed in this book are symptoms of issues that are likely to persist long after their details of specific cases are forgotten. I am completing this draft at the start of 2019, during a period of unprecedented political turmoil in Britain. In the weeks that pass between the final draft and publication day, and in the years following that, the situation will further evolve. Even if the ebb and flow of historical change may date this book to a particular moment in time, the underlying themes of the book are unlikely to become anachronistic for some time to come. Fundamentally, this book concerns how we live together in diverse societies. That is not a new issue.

CHAPTER ONE

What on Earth is Going On?

Once, we knew what antisemitism was. Once, *I* knew what antisemitism was.

Not that antisemitism has been a major presence in my own life. Once, as a boy, I was at the local swimming pool when another kid asked me "where's your Jew cap?" and "is your Jew cap in the post?". I swam away and that was that, unnerved but not crushed. I didn't wear identifiably Jewish clothing, I lived a comfortable middle-class suburban life in an area thronged with Jews and attended a 50% Jewish private school. Of course, at synagogue and in Jewish youth groups I learned about the Holocaust and about contemporary antisemitism. This was all luridly horrific, but really antisemitism was something that happened to other Jews.

So profound was my lack of personal experience of antisemitism, that I found it easy to be insouciant about it. At a Jewish summer camp in my early teens I cried and cried after a Holocaust memorial ceremony, but only to draw attention to myself and get a lingering hug from a youth leader I had a crush on. At university, a Jewish friend and I fantasised about starting a Jewish Nazi skinhead band that would ironically deny the Holocaust (I later found out that there is, in fact a Jewish band called Jewdriver, who perform covers of the neo-Nazi band Skrewdriver). On a trip to Egypt in my twenties, another Jewish friend and I asked in every bookshop we could find whether they had a copy of *The Protocols of the Elders of Zion* (no, they didn't). In 1999 I thrilled to Anal Cunt's album *It Just Gets Worse*, which included songs such as "I Sent Concentration Camp Footage to America's Funniest Home Videos" and "Hitler Was a Sensitive Man". The latter contained the immortal line, "If Hitler was alive today, he'd listen to the Cure, the Smiths and Depeche Mode".

My generation of smugly secure British Jews had this luxury. Yet for all my snotty insensitivity, there was a degree of justification to the way I refused a negative Jewish identity. I didn't want to be defined by antisemites and I didn't want the magnificent, exasperating, bewildering history of what it means to be Jewish to come down to the Holocaust. I didn't want to be Jewish simply to fulfil Emil Fackenheim's "614th commandment" that "Thou shalt not hand Hitler a posthumous victory". My generation would proudly build Jewish life, aware of the past but not bound to it.

While I still feel that Jewish life has to be about more than fighting antisemites and remembering the Holocaust, over time the presence of antisemitism has loomed much larger in my life. Having children certainly changed me. I remember re-reading Art Spiegelman's graphic novel *Maus* when my son was a baby, and the true horror of the story hit me: the forced abandonment and subsequent death of Spiegelman's father's first-born son in Poland during the Holocaust.

What changed me most of all has been my experience as a writer and scholar during the last fifteen or so years. I began participating in debates about Israel and antisemitism in the early 2000s. In online comment threads, at events I have spoken at within and without the Jewish community, I've been unable to avoid the tumultuous anger and passion that accompanies this issue. It has become impossible not to be embroiled in controversies over antisemitism. And as someone with friends and contacts across the divide, it has become increasingly difficult to resist the siren song of those who would seek to have me in their camp.

I also started to notice the depth of conflict *between* Jews over antisemitism as I researched the divisions over Israel in Diaspora Jewish communities for my 2014 book *Uncivil War: The Israel Conflict in the Jewish Community*. So often, Jewish divisions over Israel were inextricably linked to different Jewish views on antisemitism. In fact, part of what makes divisions over Israel so toxic is the perception that some Jews are inviting, excusing or exacerbating antisemitism.

From January 2015, following attacks on Jewish targets in Copenhagen and Paris, things got even more fraught. At events I spoke at and in interviews I gave, everyone wanted to ask the same questions: Is antisemitism getting worse? Are Jews still safe in Europe? What is causing violence against Jews? And what can be done about it?

Then there was the election of Jeremy Corbyn as Labour Party leader in September 2015. Many Jews I know and respect viewed the accession to the leadership of a man they consider to be tolerant of antisemitism with fear and horror. Other Jews I know and respect were thrilled to have an unabashedly socialist leader who would challenge Israeli crimes. As the Labour Party controversy exploded and antisemitism became an issue of national importance in the UK, there was no longer any way of avoiding it.

I have been on an ironic kind of journey. When antisemitism was a marginal issue in my life, I was absolutely clear what it was. I may have refused to be defined by it, I may have even chosen to make light of it, but I knew how to recognise it: Antisemitism was deranged, violent hatred against Jews. Today, antisemitism is an issue with which I am constantly engaged, something that dominates my life. But even when I am sure what it is, it doesn't always present itself as deranged, violent hatred. And the implications for my life and that of other Jews are unclear.

The Strangeness of Contemporary Antisemitism

Antisemitism has become *strange*.[1] It is no longer an easily recognisable phenomenon with easily recognisable implications. Look across the world right now and you find antisemitism. Or is it antisemitism? That is the question that sparks controversy.

In the UK, Jeremy Corbyn's leadership of the Labour Party has been accompanied by a continuous series of claims and counter-claims about the prevalence of antisemitism in his new-look party. Corbyn's own history of what some perceive as support for Hamas and Hezbollah is viewed with anxiety in much of the Jewish community. On- and offline statements made by party members and activists are scrutinised for antisemitic content, with many accused of having crossed the line from criticism of Israel to outright antisemitism. These accusations are fiercely rebutted with counter-accusations that the Labour right and pro-Israel groups are conspiring to bring Corbyn down through the cynical use of false allegations. Shami Chakrabarti, former head of the civil liberties campaign group Liberty, was tasked in 2016 with conducting an inquiry into antisemitism in the Labour Party and clarifying the issue.[2] She didn't succeed and was accused of whitewashing the problem.[3] The Jewish Labour vote collapsed as communal organisations held demonstrations against the party's tolerance for antisemitism.[4] A 2018 survey found that 84% of Jews said that antisemitism in political life was a very, or fairly big problem (more than in any other European country).[5] From February 2019, a succession of Jewish and non-Jewish MPs and members cited antisemitism as a major reason for leaving the Labour Party, some to join other political groupings.

Yet Jews are an important part of the Corbyn project, such as Jon Lansman, founder of the grassroots group Momentum. A new organisation, Jewish Voice for Labour, has fought back at what it sees as false accusations of antisemitism. Facing them, the non-Corbynite Jewish Labour Movement has struggled to retain its position as the only Jewish affiliated society in the party.

The American left is also accused of tolerating antisemitism. For example, the Women's March has been dogged by controversy over leading figures, such as Linda Sarsour and Tamika Mallory. Their insufficient distancing from Louis Farrakhan (in the case of Mallory) and support for boycotts of Israel (in the case of Sarsour) have been treated as antisemitic in some quarters. Jews are both defenders and prosecutors of the leading figures in the Women's March. How is it that an attempt to build unity and solidarity between women could degenerate into a morass of accusation and counter-accusation?

In the US, Donald Trump has been accused of presiding over an upsurge in antisemitism. In a statement marking Holocaust Memorial Day early in his presidency, he caused offence to many Jews by not mentioning that its victims were Jewish. In his blandly apathetic statements about the riots in Charlottesville in August 2017, he had difficulty in coming out and condemning neo-Nazis marching under the slogan "Jews will not replace us!".[6] Jew-haters on the alt right see in Trump a president who is, if not completely one of them, someone who has enabled their ideas to flourish.[7]

Yet there are Jews in the Trump White House, including his own son-in-law. Trump delighted some Jewish supporters of Israel by moving the US embassy to Jerusalem.[8] Sections of the growing orthodox Jewish minority in the US see Trump as an ally in their quest for "religious freedom" (to discriminate).[9]

On campus, an ongoing struggle over antisemitism, pro-Palestinian activism and free speech rages. At City University of New York in 2015, warring pro-Israel and pro-Palestinian factions faced off in corridors and classrooms.[10] The right-wing Zionist Organization of America went into action, accusing the university of harbouring antisemitism. The New York State Senate threatens to cut the university's funding for tolerating antisemitism. When demonstrators shouted "Zionists out of CUNY" did they mean "Jews out of CUNY"?

Throughout Europe, antisemitism is a pressing issue. A 2018 survey found that 90% of Jews in twelve European countries (including the UK) felt that antisemitism was increasing in their country.[11] Jews in France, Belgium and

Denmark have been singled out for murder and harassment by Islamist militants. In France, concerns about the physical security of the community have led to a spike in emigration, a substantial proportion of it to Israel.[12] At the same time, some of their persecutors come from Muslim minorities that have themselves been marginalised and discriminated against.

Elsewhere, the resurgent authoritarian right, exemplified by Hungary's Victor Orbán, draw on familiar antisemitic tropes when targeting the likes of George Soros. At the same time, such leaders are often warmly disposed towards Israel and, sometimes at least, Israel reciprocates the love.[13] Far-right populists in the UK such as Katie Hopkins are also keen to show their love of Israel, although most Jews remain suspicious of them.[14]

Support for Israel also reaches across the divide between Jews and fundamentalist Christians in the US. The Texan Pastor John Hagee, founder of Christians United For Israel, has been given awards and accolades by US Jewish organisations and is welcomed warmly by the Israeli government. In 2007 the (Jewish) senator Joseph Lieberman described Hagee as "an *Ish Elohim*. A man of God". Hagee has also described Jewish persecution as the result of Jews' disobedience of God and the Holocaust as willed by God.[15]

And in Israel it is 1938. Again. So Israel's prime minister Benjamin Netanyahu informs the world when denouncing the Iran nuclear deal brokered with the Obama administration in 2015.[16] Once again, the Jewish people are sold out by the world and face extinction at the hands of an implacable enemy. Just as in Germany in 1938, today's helpless Jews can only look on in terror, armed with only... their own nation state, with the most powerful army in the region, backed by a nuclear arsenal.

None of this coheres into a legible picture. Who are the oppressed and who are the oppressors? Who are the persecutors and who are the persecuted? It depends on whom you ask. Different kinds of Jews in different kinds of places feel themselves to be facing different kinds of threats. Different kinds of people in different kinds of places are perpetrating those threats. There is no agreement amongst Jews or non-Jews as to what antisemitism consists of. These days, when even the bluntest Jew-hater is accused of antisemitism, the usual response is to deny it.

"Twas ever thus?" Not to this degree. While antisemitism has never been the same thing in all times and places, denying antisemitism is a much more recent, modern phenomenon. Why would you deny something that was, for much of history, commonplace and unremarkable? And the ways in which Jews today relate to the state and sources of power is broader than at any time in history. There have always been wealthy and powerful Jews and in some places Jewish life flourished. Today, the position of Jews — sometimes an embattled minority, sometimes a settled and privileged minority, sometimes a hegemonic majority — resists easy summary.

We still think we know what antisemitism is. We think of blood libels, expulsions, pogroms and — above all — the Holocaust, and then we look at antisemitism today. What we choose to see is, all too frequently, coloured by the lenses of history. Every antisemitic incident today risks either being seen as a precursor to genocide, or trivial compared to what came before.

The hatred, suspicion and fear of Jews that we have

become accustomed to over centuries — what Robert Wistrich called in his eponymous book "the longest hatred" — has broken down into a plurality of bewildering disputes.[17] The issue of antisemitism today is fought out on a battleground of mutual accusations, in which everyone claims to be the victim. The controversy that results is a ravenous beast that transforms those who enter its maw, upending political certainties and producing weird alliances.

The stranger antisemitism becomes, the greater the desperation for clarity. If we can "fix" what antisemitism is and what a Jew is, then perhaps we can find some stable ground on which to fight. This desire to find certainty exacerbates the conflict, making it more intractable. It also shrinks it down, turning the question of antisemitism into a plurality of micro-controversies, hermeneutic exercises to parse whether this tweet or that cartoon can be considered antisemitic.

So who is correct? What does antisemitism mean today? How should it be defined?

The Politics of Definition

I can't avoid it any longer. This is the point in the book where I'm supposed to tell you what I think antisemitism is. This is the point in the book where you are supposed to decide whether or not I can be trusted, whether my concerns should be listened to or not. This is the point where the conversation usually ends.

Today, when Jews speak about antisemitism, we are closely scrutinised by both Jews and non-Jews. Before we can get a hearing, listeners want to know what our agendas are, what sort of Jews we are and what our stance is on Israel. If we pass these tests, we may be given the right to define antisemitism and our assessment of its seriousness.

The politics of antisemitism today is a politics of definition. It is inevitable that the term, like any other term that describes a social problem, will need to be defined. But what sort of behaviour and what sort of person should be caught in its net? Given that many of those accused of antisemitism vociferously deny that they are antisemitic, they will inevitably gravitate towards a definition of antisemitism that doesn't include them. That also means that they will listen only to those Jews who share their own definition of antisemitism.

The disputatiousness of the definitional politics of antisemitism is not entirely new. As Kenneth Marcus argues, while the issue of Israel has intensified definitional controversies in recent years, defining antisemitism has always been enmeshed in complex ideological disputes:

> Definitional controversies, while always present in the study and discourse surrounding anti-Semitism, have increased in the years following the onset of the Second Intifada, because scholars, practitioners, and activists need a generally accepted means of distinguishing between anti-Semitism and the various offences that are directed at Israel or at Jews who support Israel but that do not merit that designation. This is true today for the same reason that it has long been true: because definitions are fraught with ideological assumptions that divide schools of thought.[18]

Disputes over the definition of antisemitism are not simply something that prevent us from tackling the "real" problem — they are part of the problem. Indeed, when some Jews find that their definition of antisemitism is not accepted, they can experience this itself as antisemitic.

The problem of the definition of antisemitism is baked into the word itself. One ubiquitous online trope that appears whenever the question of antisemitism is raised, points out the problems with the term. Take this example, forwarded to me by a friend from a Facebook comment thread in spring 2018:

> Semites are a race of people that includes many different types of people including Christians, Muslims, Jews (and even many sensible people who see through the ridiculousness of religion.) The "Jews" are not a "race" as many try to claim.

A variant of this trope excludes Jews from the Semitic category altogether, as in these two examples forwarded to me from a June 2018 Twitter thread (in all their uncorrected glory):

> The israelites today have no claim to this land they descended from turns they are ashkenazi jews meaning they simply adopted the religion but are not semites, they have NO 3,000 year history in this region

> Palestinians are Semites, if you are against palestinians you are the anti semitic filth. And also, I'm not against Jews, religion doesn't matter for me :)

Such comments assume that Jews define themselves as "Semites" and define antisemitism as anything that opposes them. They assume that in defining themselves in this way, Jews have sought to exclude other groups from the Semitic category, particularly the Palestinians. They also assume that Jews have no connection to the Middle East. Indeed, they are not to be put into the ethnic/racial category at all, being a religion only.

Definitions of antisemitism are closely connected to definitions of Jews. There is a kind of violence in shoe-horning Jews into a category — "religion" — that Jews did not create themselves and, indeed, was developed long after the genesis of the Jewish people. There is a parallel here to the way the term Islamophobia is rejected by arguing that Islam is "only a religion" and as such, criticism cannot be confused with racism. Indeed, to even insist that there is such thing as Islamophobia is to cunningly attempt to prevent legitimate discussion of Islam.

I've never met a Jew who defines themselves as a "Semite", other than ironically. In fact, Semite was a term imposed on us in the modern era. The term was popularised by a proud self-confessed German antisemite Wilhelm Marr, when he founded the "League of Antisemites" in 1879. Historically, the term Jews generally used to refer to what became known as antisemitism was *Sinat Yisrael* ("hatred of [the people of] Israel"), although this is now uncommon. More recently, other terms such as "Judeophobia" have sometimes been used as alternatives, but they have only had limited traction. Antisemitism appears to be the term we are stuck with.

Inasmuch as the phenomenon of antisemitism is based on telling Jews what they really are, perhaps the Jewish adoption of the term to name the abuse they are faced with could be interpreted as a subversive gesture. I follow the common practice of spelling the word as antisemitism rather than anti-Semitism, in order to emphasise that there is no such thing as "Semitism". In a similar way, to adopt the term anti-racist is to subvert the idea that "races" exist, while still recognising the existence of prejudice based on a belief that races exist.

Even if there were such things as Semites and those Semites were exclusively Jews, it isn't clear what it means to be "anti" them. Believing that all of them should be exterminated? Believing that they should be restricted from public life or expelled? Or simply not liking them very much? And who are antisemites against? Those Jews in their own country? All Jews everywhere? Or only certain kinds of Jews?

Such questions and ambiguities have led the historian David Nirenberg to favour the term "Anti-Judaism".[19] He has pointed out the ways in which antisemitism is a sub-set of a much broader phenomenon. Throughout most of Jewish history, anti-Judaism has been a "powerful theoretical framework for making sense of the world" and "a pedagogical fear that gives enduring form to some of the key concepts and questions in the history of thought". Above all, Jews persistently *matter*, even in cultures with no Jews living amongst them.

The term antisemitism is used in multiple different ways by different people at different times. Some scholars have argued that the application of antisemitism to a disparate set of phenomena that occurred in widely varying contexts is ahistorical and does not help in understanding those phenomena.[20] The term has a history, which reflects changing phenomena that have been understood in different ways. As David Feldman has argued, the argument that antisemitism is a deep-seated and unchanging phenomenon is relatively recent; at one point the term only tended to be applied to specifically modern forms of antipathy to Jews.[21]

Somehow, in order to act in the world we have to find some way to suture antisemitism's diverse meanings into a workable form that will allow us to identify and tackle abuse, prejudice and hatred directed against Jews. The contingencies of political action and self-defence demand clarity. Inevitably, to define antisemitism clearly will be to erase complexity. It is a project that is simultaneously necessary and doomed to never quite succeed.

This contorted mix of urgency and failure has permeated the UK Labour Party's attempts to address antisemitism. Its attempts to produce a workable definition of antisemitism are a case study in the definitional politics of antisemitism.

From the spring to the autumn of 2018, the British Labour Party tore itself apart in an effort to produce clarity on antisemitism. As the party worked to overhaul its disciplinary procedures, creaking under the strain of complaints of antisemitism, it sought to adopt a definition of antisemitism that could be applied to those cases. There was no disagreement that a definition was necessary, but there were deep divisions over what it should include and exclude.

The divisive question was where the line between criticism of Israel/Zionism and antisemitism should be drawn. UK Jewish communal organisations and the Jewish

Labour Movement (which is affiliated to the Labour Party and broadly upholds the Labour Zionist political tradition) advocated the party's adoption of the working definition of antisemitism developed by the International Holocaust Remembrance Alliance (IHRA).[22] The IHRA definition has been widely, although far from universally, adopted by organisations and governments around the world. However, pro-Palestinian activists, together with Jewish non-Zionist activists and organisations, argued that IHRA treats legitimate political criticism of Israel and Zionism as antisemitic. To its detractors, the use of the IHRA definition would inevitably drag in people who are entirely innocent of antisemitism and inhibit pro-Palestinian activism. To its defenders, IHRA would provide Jews protection from an antisemitism that takes the form of anti-Zionism and opposition to Israel.

In early July 2018, Labour's National Executive Committee (NEC) adopted a code of conduct over antisemitism based on the IHRA's.[23] It also subtracted, added to and clarified some of the examples of antisemitism that the IHRA highlighted. Many of the changes were made in response to criticisms that the IHRA would inhibit or even prohibit pro-Palestinian activism. For example, the NEC code stated:

> Discourse about international politics often employs metaphors drawn from examples of historic misconduct. It is not antisemitism to criticise the conduct or policies of the Israeli state by reference to such examples unless there is evidence of antisemitic intent.[24]

This is a clear reference to the use of Nazi comparisons to Israel and Zionism, which regularly cause distress to Jews. The code argued that such comparisons might not be antisemitic in cases where there is no antisemitic "intent". Here and elsewhere in the code, a consideration of intent is a key dividing line with the IHRA, which does not mention it. Indeed, most methods of monitoring racism do not mention intent. For those who suffer it, the intent behind racist abuse is less important than the fact of the racist abuse.

In the outcry from Jewish leaders and organisations that followed the publication of the code, the introduction of intent into the definition of antisemitism was a key criticism. It appeared to give a get-out clause to anyone accused of antisemitism by allowing them to argue that they acted in good faith. As the controversy continued, it became clear that the adoption of a definition *not* of the Labour Party's own making would be a precondition for gaining the trust of mainstream Jewish community leaders and organisations, as well as the Jewish Labour Movement. Conversely, the adoption of the IHRA definition would alienate sections of the Labour left, pro-Palestinian activists and Jewish anti-Zionists. The IHRA and alternative definitions became more than simply ways of defining antisemitism, they became texts that defined both freedom from hate and freedom of expression.

The NEC was obliged to announce a consultation on the new code. In the run up to the NEC meeting at the start of September that would decide the code's fate, rhetoric heated up. A letter to the *Independent* from a collection of migrant and Black, Asian and Minority (BAME) groups argued that the IHRA definition would prohibit discussion of the injustices that have befallen the Palestinians and, in doing so, would contribute to the dangerous rise in racism in society generally.[25] To support the IHRA definition would be to support racism

When the NEC met on 4 September to decide on the definition, angry demonstrations for and against the definition faced off against each other (with Jews on both sides). The NEC's eventual decision to adopt the full IHRA definition did not in itself abate Jewish anger against Corbyn and the Labour Party for letting this situation happen. Pro-Palestinian activists responded by tweeting incendiary rhetoric against Israel with the hashtag #DefyIHRA. As subsequent events showed, this was not the end of the controversy.

Amidst this bitter conflict, it was easy to lose sight of a widespread consensus that united both sides: That the two rival codes had a clear and fixed meaning that could only ever be interpreted in one way. This shows an almost touching faith in the possibility that a short document could conclusively pin down what a complex and multi-faceted phenomena like antisemitism actually is.

IHRA is actually much more ambiguous than it has often been characterised. Take, for example, the IHRA's response to the issue of whether opposition to the existence of Israel as a Jewish state is antisemitic or not. The definition lists a number of examples of what antisemitism could consist of, including:

> Denying the Jewish people their right to self-determination, e.g., by claiming that the existence of a State of Israel is a racist endeavor.[26]

Does this mean that accepting the right of self-determination in principle but denying it in practice (by saying that in current historical circumstances a Jewish state cannot exist without being oppressive) is antisemitic? Would the reverse also be antisemitic (accepting Israel's *de facto* continued existence as a Jewish state but saying that a Jewish state would in principle be wrong)? What about arguing that the state of Israel is a racist state now but wasn't always or doesn't have to be in the future?

Definitions of antisemitism are made by human beings, with all the fallibility that that implies. Even in its own terms, the IHRA definition is a "working" definition. Cogent criticisms of the definition have been made that are not based on a denial of left antisemitism.[27] Its critics have helped to highlight the contingent and messy circumstances out of which it was created.[28] Yet in the midst of controversies over the definition of antisemitism, the IHRA has been treated as a monolith, unyielding and absolute, for good and for ill.

Too often, in struggles over antisemitism, there is an odd sort of collusion going on; that acceptance or rejection of a definition will allow you to win or lose. In some respects that is true, to the extent that if legal, political and institutional authorities adopt a particular definition it can have very real consequences. On a pragmatic level, we cannot do without definitions of antisemitism. Indeed, for some purposes, such as monitoring of hate crimes, they are essential. That they do not attract unanimity is unfortunate but not a reason to abandon them altogether.

Yet definitions of antisemitism cannot tell us the whole truth about antisemitism. The swirling, fluctuating nature of social reality is such that categorisations of any phenomena risk missing something or, alternatively, over-interpreting. The sociologist Howard Garfinkel argued that phenomena "escape" when pinned down by modes of "formal analysis" abstracted from the context in which they are embedded.[29] While definitions of social phenomena might be useful means to particular ends, they inevitably leave something missing, something that cannot be easily reconstructed.

Even when certain definitions come to dominate in particular spheres, those who do not hold to them do not simply disappear and not all of them are antisemites. In fact, much of the hurt incurred in the current controversy is to those whose understanding and experience of antisemitism is ruled illegitimate yet who still linger, like a ghost at the feast. When Jews are told that their perceptions of antisemitism do not fit the convenient definition — as when Jews are told that anti-Zionism is never antisemitic — that in itself can be experienced as antisemitism. When non-Jews are treated as antisemitic when they sincerely believe themselves to be merely anti-Zionist, that can go against their most treasured sense of themselves as anti-racist to the core.

I don't believe that all accusations and denials of antisemitism are necessarily justifiable or unjustifiable. I don't believe that all definitions of antisemitism are equally good or bad. I don't believe that just because we disagree on a particular subject we should just give up on it. I do have a strong sense of what antisemitism is or isn't, bolstered by my academic engagement with the subject.

The problem is that when I or anyone else defines their terms in advance of discussing antisemitism, it has the effect of terminating any possibility of communicating with those who do not agree with them. Yet how can change come without communicating across boundaries?

Where I Stand

I do have boundaries and red lines. Open and convinced antisemites — the ones who "everyone" agrees should be defined as antisemites — cannot be gently persuaded into abandoning antisemitism, at least not by me. What I am concerned with is finding a way to speak to those who might be seen as antisemitic by *somebody's* definition, but not by all. This is the liminal zone in which, if there is any possibility of movement in a stuck controversy, at least some of the change will have to come.

What I want to do, therefore, is to open up this liminal zone. One of the problems with the term antisemitism and its definitional politics is that it turns broader questions of how to relate to Jews into a classificatory exercise. Too often, this creates an absolute boundary between the antisemitic and the non-antisemitic. Such a boundary risks ignoring behaviours and attitudes that are problematic but do not meet the definitional standard of antisemitism.

So this is where I stand: When I use the term antisemitism without further qualification in this book, I am referring to what I will call "consensus antisemitism". Consensus antisemitism is the non-liminal, easily-identifiable antisemitism that falls inside the vast majority of definitions. This is open, unashamed, visceral hatred, disdain or abuse directed at Jews as Jews (although consensus antisemites still might refuse the label antisemite for reasons discussed in the next chapter). It may be expressed through clear statements of hatred, through violence, through discrimination. It may take the form of conspiracy theories, fantasies of Jewish evil and the like. Consensus antisemitism is closely related to racism more generally, but has its own characteristics. Where appropriate, I treat antisemitism as a form of racism, at other points I treat them as distinct.

That's the easy bit.

While I am not suggesting that consensus antisemitism is the sum total of all antisemitism, I will not be drawn into the vortex of defining the boundaries of antisemitism beyond it. That is sometimes a necessary exercise — particularly for the purpose of monitoring, research and regulation — and I have views on how to do it. It's just that I'm not going to do it in this book, regardless of the need to do it in other books (or, for that matter, in articles I myself have written in the past and may write in the future).

Instead, I will range beyond the consensus into the broader, liminal zone of selective anti/semitism. The crucial difference between consensus antisemitism and selective anti/semitism is that the former does not seek Jewish approval; it has no place for anything other than the occasional, highly exceptional, Jew within it. Consensus antisemitism is indifferent to who Jews actually are what they actually believe, sometimes entirely ignorant of them. The nexus of politics and identity is not a problem for consensus antisemites as there is no politics that Jews could hold that would "save" them. Consensus antisemitism is directed at *all* Jews and has no interest in Jewish diversity; it assumes that Jews themselves form a consensus. When

Robert Bowers opened fire on worshippers at the Tree of Life Synagogue in Pittsburgh on 27 October 2018, he shouted "All Jews must die" — as clear a statement of consensus antisemitism as you will find. Although not all consensus antisemites want all Jews dead, they do wish ill on all Jews, not just a fraction.

In contrast, selective anti/semitism is intensely interested in and even knowledgeable about who Jews are and, in particular, what politics they hold. Selective anti/semites seek out Jews for approval or damnation; they make alliances with Jews and hold them close.

This zone of selective anti/semitism is a confused and confusing jumble of love and hate for different kinds of Jews, a space of support for and opposition to Jewish political projects. In the zone, Jews are a fascination, an obsession, a puzzle to be solved. The zone extends across the boundaries of most definitions of antisemitism. By refusing to be held within those boundaries we can become aware of the wider prevalence of negative attitudes and behaviours towards Jews of any kind, in the widest sense, whether these attitudes are seen as negative by all Jews or by only a fraction. Bewilderment, disappointment and incomprehension of Jews are as significant as outright hatred. Some of this meets the standards of some definitions of antisemitism and some of it does not. In widening my focus in this way, I am attempting to raise questions about how it might or might not be possible to relate negatively to the nexus of Jewish politics and Jewish identity. While I may not promiscuously indict people of antisemitism, I will be catching a much wider population in a much bigger net.

Amongst the people caught up in the zone are some of those on the left who have been accused of antisemitism. My contention is that consensus antisemitism is much less common on the left than on the right. What is much more common on the left is the mixture of bafflement, fascination, admiration, repulsion and — above all — selectivity that constitutes selective anti/semitism. To accuse someone who is caught up in selective anti/semitism of being an antisemite, pure and simple, is to ignore their ambivalence. Selective anti/semites are trying to love some Jews at the same time that other Jews are accusing them of hating them — and vice versa.

The fact that selective anti/semitism is not "pure" hatred makes the zone that it occupies one from which movement is possible. From within that space it is easy to drift into consensus antisemitism. Maybe it is also easy to fall out of, back into a more thoroughgoing anti-racism. This is where hope lies. Some readers may accuse me of promiscuously indicting too wide a range of people of selective anti/semitism. But I hope that my indictments are different in tone and intent to other accusations of antisemitism that they are commonly made.

Now for the thing that some UK readers will have been impatient for me to come clean on: I do think that Jeremy Corbyn, like others on the left and within the pro-Palestinian movement, has sometimes strayed into the zone of selective anti/semitism, but I am not suggesting that he has a heart full of hate for Jews and that his professed anti-racism is nothing more than a lie. I don't see his wanderings into the zone as particularly remarkable or extraordinary. It is easy to drift into selectivity out of bewilderment, ignorance and blindness. And it may be easy to drift out again too. The question is how to leave selective anti/semitism behind permanently. That is harder, but not impossible.

While I do make space for hope, the problem remains serious. Consensus antisemitism is not necessarily more severe than selective anti/semitism. Even if there is more hope to be found in the possibility of movement away from selective anti/semitism than consensus antisemitism, both variants may draw on similar discourses and tropes. Antisemitism of any kind is not a fixed, uniform way of seeing the world. In a ground-breaking survey of British attitudes to Jews and Israel released in 2017, the Institute for Jewish Policy Research proposed an "elastic view" of antisemitism.[30] The authors suggested that, rather than being a single attitude towards Jews, antisemitism is expressed through multiple attitudes and only a hardcore minority hold them all. It is perfectly possible for a consensus antisemite to hold only one antisemitic attitude and a selective anti/semite to hold multiple ones — the difference is that the former will apply these attitudes to Jews uniformly and the latter will apply them to a sub-set. For example, an obsession with the pernicious power of "the Rothschilds" may be applied to all Jews or just to "Rothschild Zionists". Whereas consensus antisemites speak of "the Jew", selective anti/semites speak of "Jews".

In any case, consensus antisemitism and selective anti/semitism are not hermetically sealed compartments. Many Jews experience and respond to selective anti/semitism as if it were identical to consensus antisemitism. And, as I will show later in the book, even those Jews who do not feel themselves to be impacted by selective anti/semitism or do not recognise its existence may ultimately be affected by it.

Selective anti/semites may empower consensus antisemites, whether they want to or not. As we have seen recently with the US far-right, "mainstream" political figures may create an environment conducive to more violent and less selective extremism. Sometimes, selective anti/semites may attempt to mitigate or qualify their opposition to the actions of their more extreme, consensually antisemitic relations. For selective anti/semites, consensus antisemitism of one sort may be treated as a terrible, isolated event with no wider relevance. When a George Soros-obsessed far-right terrorist attacks Jews, the selectively anti/semitic right usually condemn it, but they rarely recognise that they are complicit in the overarching discourse through their own condemnation of Soros. When a European Islamist attacks a Jewish target, pro-Palestinian selective anti/semites will offer condemnation of the lukewarm or passionate kind, but they often see it as a different category of antisemitism to the full-blooded fascist kind.

People can change. While, as I have said, it is perfectly possible for occasional visitors to selective anti/semitic zones to journey back out again, perhaps permanently, the reverse is also true. Selective anti/semitism can be a way station towards full-blooded consensus antisemitism. The growing crossover space between far-right and far-left consensus antisemitism can be accessed via multiple pathways. A starting point of empathy, concern for the oppressed and horror of war can lead eventually to a place of hatred. Some anti-war, pro-Palestinian activists such as Kenneth O'Keefe have taken meandering journeys from opposition to the Iraq war, through 9/11 conspiracy theories, towards flirtation with Holocaust denial and denunciations of the insidious power of the Jew. Former Democrat Congress-woman and Green Party presidential candidate Cynthia McKinney started off as a supporter of the Palestinians, a campaigner against the Iraq war, and ended up attending conferences with Holocaust deniers.[31] Alice Walker started off a civil rights activist, became a pro-Palestinian activist and now writes poems echoing longstanding far-right paranoia about the Talmud.[32]

This fluidity, in an age where communication has never been easier and identities never more malleable, means that it makes little sense to treat one part of the related zones of consensus antisemitism and selective anti/semitism as being *a priori* more serious than another part. If we have learned anything from the last few years it should be that history takes surprising twists and turns. It was only recently that far-right antisemitism was widely seen as a marginal, if unpleasant problem. Now, we see US Republican candidates for political office denying the Holocaust and leaders of the party repeating, barely modified, longstanding far-right talking points about Jews ushering in immigrants to replace the noble white race.[33] Who knows what tomorrow will bring? It makes sense to treat the apparently minor forms of selective anti/semitism with the same seriousness we treat the apparently severe ones.

The same argument applies to the relative importance of antisemitism compared to other racisms. Again, the insta-bility of the times is such that it is unwise to see some racisms as more serious than others. I don't think that we can be certain as to which groups racists will target and in what order, now and in the future. The opportunism of the far-right, which has recently seen Islamophobia prioritised over antisemitism in some quarters, means that no group can ever be sure when or if they will rise or fall in the pecking order of hatred.

If there ever was a time to take all racisms seriously — against any group, coming from any part of the political spectrum, however apparently minor — it is now. Yet individual books cannot do everything, and we all have to start from somewhere. My particular interest in the selective anti/semitism of the left is not a statement of disinterest in other forms of antisemitism and other forms of racism. It's a way into a complex field, pushing at its most sensitive point, the place where anti-racism begins to fail. If we are to respond to any and all racisms, there is a value in beginning at the *least* consensual point.

Ironically though, the starting point in understanding selective anti/semitism and the strangely hateful zone that it occupies is to appreciate the unhelpfully deep level of *agreement* between the protagonists in the antisemitism controversy. As I will argue in the following chapter, the broad consensus that antisemitism is a bad thing is central to the problem.

CHAPTER TWO

How Racism Became Unspeakable

Why would anyone deny that they are antisemitic? Why is racism seen as wrong?

Historically, distaste, suspicion or hatred of Jews and other "others" has been an unremarkable feature in many societies. While the "great" events in the history of antisemitism —, the massacre in York in 1190, the Spanish expulsion of 1492, the Kishniev pogrom in 1903 and, above all, the Holocaust — loom large in the Jewish imagination, it is the persistence of "casual", everyday antisemitism that reveals its deeper roots.

In 2005, the writer Simon Garfield published a book of extracts from the diaries of a selection of ordinary British citizens, written in the immediate post-war period.[1] The diaries were solicited by the Mass Observation project, which sought to take the temperature of public opinion, both during the war and afterwards. The value of the diaries is that they were written neither as a public document for subsequent publication, nor as a purely personal document. They occupy the borderlands between uncensored emotional expression and face-saving public rectitude and, as such, give an invaluable impression of what was seen as acceptable to say in semi-public settings.

On 20 November 1945, Maggie Joy Blunt, a writer in her mid-thirties living in Slough, reports a conversation with friends about the situation in Palestine (then under British control and with the Zionist movement pushing for independence):

> At lunch today someone mentioned the problem of Palestine. "I don't think the Jews should be forced to leave the country — let them go to Palestine if they want to." "Jews get such a financial hold on a country." "That's true — all the same, a country is nearly always better off where Jews are powerful — they may make big money, but they circulate it." "The produce much talent too." "Pity they have such unpleasant characteristics." "Only due to long years of persecution — aggressive trait has developed." "Well, we all get aggressive don't we, when we feel looked down on?"[2]

On 8 July 1946, Herbert Brush, a seventy-two-year-old retired electrical engineer from London, walked past the headquarters of the Zionist movement:

> When I was walking along Great Russell Street I noticed a crowd of people outside Zion House, and soon saw that they were all Jews, men and women. They were talking excitedly and going in and out of the house like bees to a hive, so I suppose they were cooking up something to say to the Government about Palestine. There was no mistaking the Jewish proboscis of the men, though it was not quite so apparent on the women. The Jews are always in trouble with some other nation and always will be I suppose.[3]

On 27 July 1946, Edie Rutherford, a forty-three-year-old housewife from Sheffield, reports on a conversation with her husband:

> Husband said this morning that he has only one sorrow about the Nuremberg thugs and that is that they did not exterminate the Jews before they were stopped at it. Husband went on to say Jews are parasites. That they are never found with their coats off, that they are cunning etc. I regret this wholesale condemnation of his but I know that he is sorely tried every day in his timber work by Jews.[4]

On 19 May 1947, B Charles, an antiques dealer in his mid-fifties from Edinburgh, mentions a chat he had:

> I had a very interesting conversation with a man from the Control Commission in German this morning... It seems all the stories we heard about the concentration camps in Germany were almost all true. But the only people in these camps were Jews and political prisoners. We both agreed that the Jews should be exterminated and that the political prisoners were just fools. It seems about 5,000,000 Jews were killed in Germany alone.[5]

Jews were not an obsession for any of the diarists. Their paradigmatically consensual antisemitism simply pops up occasionally in matter-of-fact comments. Nor are they politically radical, involved in fascism or sympathetic to the recently-beaten Nazi foe. It's hard to say whether the desire expressed by B Charles and Edie Rutherford's husband for the Jews to be exterminated would have translated to active support for a programme to do just that. What comes across is the permissibility of stereotyping Jews by their looks and behaviours, and of contemplating their persecution. While not all British people in the immediate post-war period would have spoken this way, these are not thrillingly transgressive comments, furtively confided.

These diaries offer a glimpse into a time when antisemitism was speakable, if not necessarily actionable. This is what Anthony Julius has called the "minor" (but not necessarily mild) antisemitism that had a quotidian presence in British life until at least the early 1960s.[6] It is rare for this kind of quotidian antisemitism to reveal itself with such stark clarity. Today, exposure of the normative antisemitism of the past is often treated as a kind of revelation of a dark embarrassing secret. The casual and not-so-casual antisemitism of figures as diverse as Richard Nixon, Roald Dahl, or T.S. Eliot as a matter of anguished debate today, as if they were not products of their times. The question of whether we can still understand them apart from their antisemitism, whether their distaste or hatred for Jews necessarily becomes their entire meaning, implies that it is possible to find a usable past entirely free from antisemitism.

As with antisemitism, so the historical ubiquity of other forms of racism are shocking today and constitute a barrier to coming to terms with our past. I was born in the early 1970s into a Britain where golliwogs adorned jam jars, where editions of Agatha Christie's *Ten Little Niggers* circulated freely, where black-upped minstrels appeared on TV and comedians still joked about "Pakis". I was also born at a time when such horrors were being actively combatted and in which more direct forms of racist violence and oppression were beginning to be confronted.

Pointing out the ubiquity of casual, quotidian racism in the recent or distant past risks smug complacency. Not only is racist talk still with us and, indeed, resurgent, but even if it were not, the cleansing of swathes of the public sphere of casual racism is not the same as cleansing society of deeper, insidious forms of racist thinking and its consequences. There is an opposite danger too: placing quotidian racism in the context of its times can risk appearing like a tepid defence of the indefensible. Casual and not-so-casual racism, flippant and not-so-flippant bigotry and other expressions of hate and distaste — none of this has ever been right. Nor is it our inevitable destiny as humans. But there is no way round the fact that throughout history it has often (or maybe even usually), been permissible to speak in disparaging ways about entire sub-sections of humanity. That is not to say that "everyone" was antisemitic or racist, nor does it mean that those who might speak in casually antisemitic or racist ways would support political programmes that would turn prejudice into persecution. It simply means that it was a possible option that could be spoken of in many circles without automatically consigning you to pariahdom.

The Shrinking of Racist Space

The casual antisemitism expressed by the diarists was to rapidly lose its normality in the post-war period. Indeed, they were already living in a world in which the boundaries of the speakable had become increasingly constrained.

This might seem a bizarre argument, given that they were writing at a time when a Western country had just carried out a systematic genocide of a people. When we think of the Nazis and antisemitism, we don't generally think of them as being constrained by anything other than the limits of their hateful imagination. But as I have argued elsewhere, even the Nazis found it exceptionally difficult to speak openly of the extermination of the Jews other than in private meetings or in whispered asides, regardless of whether they approved of it or not.[7]

The Nazis were still constrained by the process of Western modernity that, beginning in the seventeenth and eighteenth centuries, made it more difficult to argue for a politics based on open hate, greed, anger and violence. The nation states that emerged from the revolutions of the enlightenment period, as well as those that reformed themselves incrementally, were to be governed through reasoned, rational debates conducted by equal citizens. They were to eschew venality, violence and prejudice; one's place in the hierarchy was to be dictated by one's individual capacity, not birthright. Of course, such ideals were often, even usually, hypocritically pursued. The extension of the rights of modernity to women, slaves, religious and ethnic minorities, and many others was often pursued slowly or not at all. In any case, ideals of reason, freedom and democracy have never completely been embraced everywhere and at all times in the West or elsewhere. But the appearance of non-prejudiced, rational and reasonable action has become essential for political and social legitimacy.

In this context modern antisemitism had to adopt new and creative methods to uphold its legitimacy. Hatred for

Jews could no longer be a justification in and of itself, and theological arguments against the Jews began to lose credibility as politics became increasingly secularised. New justifications had to be sought in "rational", "scientific" assessments of the Jews' conspiratorial nature, their racial degeneracy, the dangers they posed to the world. When the rights of citizenship were extended to Jews, new possibilities emerged for othering Jews. Now that Jews could assimilate should they wish to, their invisibility was leveraged to create new antisemitic myths. The Jew became monstrously powerful, a hidden conspirator.

Nonetheless, with laws formally enjoining non-Jews to treat Jews as fellow citizens, antisemitism became a much more arduous pursuit. This was one of the lessons of the Dreyfus affair: the process of driving one Jew out of the French army ended up becoming mired in years of political turmoil, faked conspiracies and labyrinthine legal battles — and in the end, he was exonerated. The Holocaust also set the bar high as well; non-Nazi antisemites might have been forgiven for thinking whether it was really worth all the bother to go to such lengths to try and eliminate every single Jew. Much better to confine one's distaste for Jews to private or semi-private comments within one's own circle, to occasional asides, to keeping a wide berth from them where possible, excluding them from one's golf club and letting them live at a distrustful distance.

In places like the UK, where support for a systematic programme of antisemitism became restricted to a small far-right fringe in the post-war period, everyday antisemitism ended up withering on the vine, lacking mainstream means for operationalisation into coherent policy. Perhaps

B Charles would have signed up as a guard in an extermination camp for Jews if one were to have been set up in Edinburgh, or perhaps not. He would have known that this was unlikely and so could have enjoyed a flippant moment of fantasising about genocide without either official endorsement or condemnation.

The post-war period also saw a series of developments that were to make it even more difficult for public, acknowledged antisemitism to gain a significant foothold, in most Western countries at least. The pioneering war crimes prosecutions at Nuremberg in 1945–6 introduced the concept of "crimes against humanity" and, simultaneously, the popularisation of Raphael Lemkin's neologism of "genocide" provided an emerging language that could, legally and morally, ground a rejection of Nazi-style antisemitism. The various clauses of the 1948 Universal Declaration of Human Rights ruled out the possibility that a state could treat one class of citizens as of lesser worth than another. Its universalism, also reflected in other work of the United Nations, set up a baseline, a default position that the membership of a particular group is not cause to treat an individual as being of lesser worth. The rapid decolonisation process in the post-war period also saw Western powers lose their ability (with varying degrees of reluctance) to directly impose their will on others. Large-scale immigration to the UK and other European countries, initially from former or current colonies, pushed governments to expand who was part of the national community. Legislation such as the UK's 1965 Race Relations Act began a process through which racism and discrimination were officially recognised and combatted. In the US, the civil rights struggle saw official and semi-official barriers to African-American participation in social and political life confronted and eventually removed.

None of these developments meant that antisemitism and racism were abolished in the post-war period. But what they did mean was that the possibility of turning prejudice into a systematic and open programme of persecution or discrimination became progressively restricted and, in the process, it became even more difficult to express antipathy towards particular minority groups. Looking at 1960s speeches by racist politicians such as Enoch Powell in the UK and George Wallace in the US, we can see a kind of raging against the dying of the light; a desperate rearguard action against the closing of the space of the speakable. Similarly, the institution of the legislative and administrative paraphernalia of Apartheid in South Africa in the late 1940s was as much as anything born out of a lack of confidence that white rule could be maintained indefinitely without considerable institutional scaffolding.

Perhaps we can also see such a rearguard action in some of the controversies surrounding "political correctness" and "identity politics" that have raged since the 1980s. With the ability to argue for systematic programmes of racism now severely curtailed, there were fewer places in which one's racist desires were not frustrated. The passion with which, for example, racist stand-up comedy in the UK, or restrictive country club membership criteria in the US, were defended, demonstrates the desire to retain a space in which the delights of racist speech could be experienced. To an extent, anti-Roma racism performs this function today; where other forms of racism have been delegitimised, hating the Roma can be a last redoubt of open prejudice.[8]

The Rise of Denial

It might seem like Donald Trump and other right-wing populists have re-enabled the open expression of racism. Certainly, the relief and delight that finally someone is "saying the unsayable" is palpable amongst a significant section of the supporters of the populist right. But the logic that made racism unspeakable in the post-war period remains powerful. That racist expression is experienced as transgressively thrilling is testament to the enduring strength of the boundaries constraining racist speech. We are still a long way from a situation where the casual racism that we saw at the beginning of this chapter becomes unremarkable once again.

Even when racism speaks publicly, it is still usually bound up in disclaimers of not being racist. The practice of denial of racist intent — "I'm not racist but... " — is now deeply embedded in everyday discourse. As Eduardo Bonilla-Silva has argued, in the US racism has become "colour-blind", with a multitude of techniques used to speak of race without speaking of race.[9] A wilful "ignorance" of white implication in persistent racial hierarchies has long been a central part in their maintenance long after officially-mandated discrimination was abolished.[10]

This habit of denial even compels those on the far-right who really should embrace the identity of racist to avoid the term. "Race realist" or sometimes "racialist" are often preferred, framing racism as the disinterested recognition of what they see as irrefutable differences between races.[11] Further, they affirm the language of anti-racism when complaining about "anti-white racism" and the threat of "white genocide". This simultaneous affirmation and disavowal of racism can be absurd. The US Proud Boys movement simultaneously states that anti-racism and "Anti Racial Guilt" are central tenets, and describes the ideal Proud Boy as a "Western chauvinist who refuses to apologise for creating the modern world".[12] One of the most extraordinary examples of this simultaneity was posted on the popular blog *Boing Boing* in January 2017: A photo of the door of a pickup truck in New Mexico featuring a confederate flag with the slogans "Secede!" "Anti-Sodomy" "Common Decency" "Pro-Life" and... "Non-Racist".[13]

This drive to deny racism extends to antisemitism. Indeed, denial may actually be stronger when it comes to antisemitism. As Kenneth Marcus argues:

> Nowadays virtually everyone is opposed to anti-Semitism although no one agrees about what it means to be anti-Semitic. Indeed, it may be argued that virtually every anti-Semite today is also a professed enemy of anti-Semitism.[14]

One of the reasons for this is that, for many of those on the left who are accused of antisemitism today, the accusation is an assault on one's very identity. It is fair to assume that, for the person who painted "non-racist" on his racist truck, to be accused of racism would be annoying, but they are unlikely to view non-racism as the very core of their being. That is not the case for many of those on the left who have been accused of antisemitism in recent years. In the post-war period, the left has often been in the vanguard of the fight against racism and antisemitism. Indeed, the "new left" that began to emerge in the 1960s became increasingly focused on anti-racism as a central component of the struggle for human liberation. To call self-defined anti-racist activists antisemites is to tell them that they are not what they claim to be. This is one of the reasons why Jeremy Corbyn and others like him have had so much difficulty in dealing with the issue: it is bewildering and unsettling to be accused of traducing one's deepest-held beliefs.

Of course it is also a serious charge to call a Christian Zionist like John Hagee, who loudly proclaims his love for the Jewish people, an antisemite. But it is perhaps less wounding to dub someone an antisemite who is, at best, apathetic to other forms of racism, than it is to attack the reputation of someone who sees themselves as opposed to all racisms. Sometimes there is a poverty of low expectations when it comes to antisemitism on the political right. It's notable that many definitions of antisemitism, including the IHRA definition, are silent as to whether Christian statements that Jews are going to hell unless they convert are antisemitic or not. Inevitably though, those who proclaim themselves to have a universal standard when it comes to anti-racism are going to be scrutinised more closely.

It is also inevitable that anti-racists accused of antisemitism will draw on widely available cultural resources in order to deny those claims. We now have decades of experience in developing sophisticated discursive tools for the denial of racism, and while those on the left may not have been in the avant-garde of the creation of those tools, they are capable of taking advantage of them when needed. Which isn't to say that accusations are always fair or denials always unreasonable, but that the process of denying antisemitism may be identical regardless of how justified the accusation is.

Antisemitism controversies have therefore come to take on a by-now-familiar pattern, reminiscent of, but not identical to, other controversies over racism. As Kenneth Marcus summarises:

> Anti-Semitism tends to proceed in two stages. First, the incident occurs, whether as assault, insult, or provocation. Then, in the second stage, disputants argue about whether the incident was really anti-Semitic or whether the Jewish complainants are instead trying to smear and silence the innocent. Often the accuser is punished for the very act of alleging bias.[15]

We might add a third stage to this: someone mentions the Nazis. For it is the Nazis that were instrumental in complicating the issue of antisemitism and making it strange to us.

The Familiarity and Strangeness of the Nazis

In June 2015, a far-right groupuscule calling itself the New Dawn Party, led by the self-confessed antisemite Joshua Bonehill-Paine, announced its intention to organise a demonstration against the "Jewification" in Golders Green, a London neighbourhood with a large Jewish population. Amongst other activities, he claimed that he would be burning a copy of the Talmud (impressive, given that the Talmud is an expensive multi-volume work). In the end, the police allowed the demonstration only if it moved to central London, where it finally took place on 4 July.

The twenty or so demonstrators were heavily outnumbered by phalanxes of police and hundreds of counter-demonstrators from a motley collection of Jewish and non-Jewish groups. The neo-Nazis carried Palestinian flags, but some of their opponents were also loudly pro-Palestinian; other counter-protestors waved Israeli flags. In the run up to the demonstration there had been squabbling between one faction, Golders Green Together, which put together a multi-faith coalition to oppose it, and other Jewish groups that protested loudly as Jews alone under the Israeli flag. From anarchists seeking to "bash the fash" (and possibly the police too) and hard-right Zionists who loathed the pro-Palestinian left as much as the Nazis — everyone wanted to get in on the act. It was not a dignified spectacle.[16]

Compared to the bitter disputes that surround the antisemitism controversy most of the time, there was no disagreement that the demonstration and its participants were antisemitic. Not only were they attacking Jews in an utterly unambiguous way, they were drawing on easily-identifiable Nazi tropes and taunting Jews with the Holocaust. This broad consensus allowed a multitude of groups, Jewish and non-Jewish, to join in the fun. But it also revealed fundamental differences as to the banner under which Nazis should be fought: Secular leftist anti-fascism? Jewish nationalism? Liberal coexistence?

In a case such as this insignificant demonstration from 2015, the stakes were not that high, and its long-term impact was minimal. When the modern heirs of the Nazis spill blood and attain power, the differences within Jewish and non-Jewish communities as to how to understand and fight them become more malign. In the wake of the October 2018 synagogue shooting in Pittsburgh, there was no shortage of condemnation and little doubt expressed that it was an instance of antisemitism. Yet questions such as the responsibility of Donald Trump and the Republican Party, together with the role the Israeli government should play in commemorating the atrocity, quickly revealed the fundamental differences within the apparent consensus.

Although the Nazis provide a common moral baseline across many societies today, this consensus isn't necessarily helpful, not least in the fight against antisemitism. Part of the reason for the consensus lies in the unusual breadth of the coalition who fought in the Second World War, which included liberal democracies, communist states and totalitarian autocracies. The comprehensiveness of the victory, the enormous blood and treasure spent in achieving it, and the savagery of the Nazis themselves ensures that the war has dominated the post-war national identities of the victors. Formulas such as the UK's "finest hour", the US's "greatest generation" and the former Soviet Union's "Great Patriotic War" all attest to this. Many of the countries that were occupied have also found ways to join in this national myth-making, emphasising heroic resistance as in France, or the rescue of Jews as in Denmark. Even Germany finds comfort in venerating those, such as Sophie Scholl, who resisted the Nazis. Who wants to be on the other side of this intimidating consensus?

The Nazis did not openly proclaim themselves to be evil. The Holocaust — like other genocides — involved the expression of transgressive, orgiastic violence, that deliberately erased or blurred the boundaries of conventional morality.[17] At the same time, even if mass murder represented the inevitable *telos* of years of violent rhetoric against and persecution of Jews, the gas chambers and *Einsatzgruppen* were not publicly acknowledged and celebrated. Part of the reason for this was undoubtedly pragmatic, as discretion smoothed the wheels of genocide by encouraging in its victims an illusory hope as to their ultimate fate. Similarly, the post-war denials of senior and not-so-senior Nazis as to their degree of knowledge of the Holocaust was as much as anything a form of self-defence against legal proceedings. But there was also a point where the Nazis desire to destroy the Jews was a desire that could not fully be acknowledged. The transgressiveness of the act could not be embraced in its entirety. Even those who were directly implicated in the Holocaust and could no longer deny it often emphasised that, even in the midst of the slaughter, they retained a sense of order, both moral and bureaucratic. Take the following exchange between Franz Stangl, the commandant of Treblinka, and his post-war interviewer Gitta Sereny:

> *"You've been telling me about your routines", I said to him. "But how did you feel? Was there anything you enjoyed, you felt good about?"*

> "It was interesting to me to find out who was cheating," he said. "As I told you, I didn't care who it was; my professional ethos was that if something wrong was going on, it had to be found out. That was my profession; I enjoyed it. It fulfilled me. And yes, I was ambitious about that; I won't deny that."[18]

Even in the midst of a catastrophic collapse of moral order, Stangl, like many others in his position, focused on those areas where he could find that order, in this case by rooting out corruption amongst his henchmen and victims. Maybe there was simply no way of reconciling the transgressive act of genocide with the desire to be a good person. Maybe the Nazis were more like "us" than we think.

Whatever the reason, the routine response to the Holocaust amongst those who should have celebrated it was to deny that it had happened. Holocaust denial became normative in the post-war world among neo-Nazis and overt antisemites. While Holocaust denial offers its own antisemitic pleasures given the pain it causes to Jews, it is primarily an attempt to retain a pristine image not just of the Nazis, but of antisemitism itself. It is ultimately a failure of nerve, a refusal to embrace the transgression that any attempt to bring about a final solution to the Jewish problem would entail.

Holocaust denial is also a reminder that the attempt to kill all Jews is, to a degree, an anomalous part of the history of antisemitism. The Nazis drew deeply from the well of pre-existing antisemitic fantasies and practices, but they also went much further. Most upsurges of antisemitism ended with Jews expelled from a particular territory, or with many killed and a remnant left alive, or with ghettoisation and legal restrictions. The Final Solution, as it evolved during the course of the Second World War, meant not just the killing or the elimination through labour of Jews that happened to be present in the territories the Nazis controlled. It also meant proactive policy-making to ensure that the net would be progressively extended until all Jews were caught in it. In July 1942, for instance, Himmler visited Finland in an (unsuccessful) attempt to persuade that government, which was fighting the Soviets alongside Germany, to hand over its two thousand Jews. The numbers were only a tiny fraction of the millions currently under Nazi control elsewhere in Europe — who were an enormous challenge to "process" as it was — and the logistics of the proposed deportation, to say nothing of the time involved in adding to Himmler's many responsibilities, revealed an obsessive desire to kill all Jews that went far beyond anything seen before in the history of antisemitism.

Alon Confino has suggested that the elimination of the Jews by the Nazis was part of a radical attempt to completely re-order history in their image:

> For the Nazis and other Germans, Jews represented time, symbolising evil historical origins that had to be eradicated for Nazi civilisation to arise [...] By persecuting and exterminating the Jews, the Nazis eliminated the shackles of a past tradition and its morality; thus making it possible to liberate their imagination, to open up new emotional, historical, and moral horizons that enabled them to imagine and create their empire of death.[19]

It is uncertain, though, how far this radical vision of a world without Jews was widely shared or, if it was, how many Germans or Nazis were really prepared to shoulder the considerable burdens required to enact it. In any case, have most antisemites really ever wanted a world without Jews? Jews are useful as a scapegoat, as an explanation for all that is wrong with the world, or simply a legitimately hateable form of human. Who would want to do without us?

Post-war antisemitism has returned to being "sustainable", in that it does not demand enormous organisational efforts and allows for the indefinite continuity of a convenient hate-object. Yet the Holocaust has also been a considerable boon to antisemites, even if most of them want to distance themselves from it. The excessive quality of the Holocaust is such that it can render other expressions of antisemitism inconsequential. When the Holocaust is treated, as it often is, as a prototypical rather than exceptional incidence of antisemitism, contemporary antisemitism can be difficult to recognise. This is not entirely unique to Jews. Any people that have suffered catastrophes may find it difficult to gauge the seriousness of other, less catastrophic racisms. Those of African descent whose ancestors were trafficked in the slave trade can sometimes struggle to articulate contemporary concerns without the temptation to conflate them with the sufferings experienced by their ancestors.

It is, in part, due to a fear of triviality that Nazi comparisons are so frequent in Jewish discourse about antisemitism. For example, in interviews with Jewish witnesses to a violent demonstration held in Paris against the conflict in Gaza in July 2014, the ghosts of the Nazi era were swiftly invoked:

> A synagogue was attacked, along with a Jewish owned grocery store. "They were shouting: 'Death to Jews,' and 'Slit Jews' throats,'" a Jewish sound engineer told London's Sunday Times. The man had lived in the community for 49 years, but when the Times reporter recently asked for his full name, he demurred. The chants, he said, "took us back to 1938."[20]

In debates about whether Jews should leave Europe due to rising antisemitism, the example of those who could not or would not leave Germany in the 1930s are ever-present.[21] Benjamin Netanyahu and others have also invoked the spectre of "1938" in calls for action against Iran.[22] While such analogies may not be credible historically speaking, they express a secret anxiety that if one were to concede that the position of the Jews today with regard to their enemies is vastly superior compared to the 1930s, Jewish fears and grievances would not be listened to.

Oh God, He's Going to Mention Godwin's Law Now Isn't He?

Even as contemporary antisemitism risks triviality in comparison to the Holocaust, the Holocaust itself is in danger of being, if not trivialised, then certainly relegated to a lazy signifier for absolute evil. One of the paradoxes of the consensus surrounding the Nazis is that, the more routinely they are invoked, the less of an impact they have.

This is widely known. Indeed, I am fully aware that at this point I am lapsing into predictability by mentioning

"Godwin's Law", coined by the American writer and lawyer Mike Godwin in 1990. The law that states that "As an online discussion grows longer, the probability of a comparison involving Hitler approaches 1".[23] Yet how could it not? So embedded is the Hitler/Nazi comparison in modern society that as early as 1951, the philosopher Leo Strauss felt compelled to coin the term *reductio ad Hitlerum*, arguing that "A view is not refuted by the fact that it happens to have been shared by Hitler".[24]

The fact that comparisons to Hitler and the Nazis are widely recognised to be cliché at the very least, does not mean that the underlying dynamic that leads to such comparisons to be made is any less problematic. Gabriel Rosenfeld has argued that the Nazi past is becoming progressively "normalised"; removed from its status as an exceptional, uniquely horrific event.[25] This normalisation is generated by everything from historians' attempts to treat the Holocaust as just another genocide, to competitive attempts to prove that one's own victimhood is comparable to that of the Jews, to the ubiquity of humorous Hitler memes online. Normalisation is met by competing attempts to reassert the exceptionality of Hitler and the Nazis, in a circular controversy that Rosenfeld refers to as the "dialectic of normalisation".

Rosenfeld does not give sufficient attention to the non-dialectical consensus that Hitler and the Nazis *matter* today and/or historically. Even to assert that the Nazis do not deserve a unique place in the pantheon of evil is to recognise that the fact they have been placed there today is of enormous significance. In a bewildering world, taking a stance on the Nazis provides a way of grounding oneself.

The more energy is spent on engaging with the Nazis and their legacy, in whatever form, the more their ubiquity spreads, to the point where the Nazis can no longer just be the Nazis. They, and everything they did, become something to argue about, something to laugh at, something to be horrified by — and maybe, ultimately, something to be bored by. One of the reasons why I, like many others, dread the imminent demise of the last survivors of the Holocaust is that they are living reminders that the Nazis actually existed, that they were not simply a trope. In fact, I also dread the passing of the last Nazis too, for the same reasons. In the absence of living individuals, it will take a special effort of will to breach the routinised ways in which we often engage with this period. When the Holocaust is simply a symbol for evil, its visceral horror threatens to escape.

It may be that more morally ambivalent responses to the Holocaust might ensure that it retains its power to disturb. Matthew Boswell has identified what he describes as a productive "Holocaust impiety" in works such as the Sex Pistols' song "Belsen Was a Gas" and Robert Littell's novel *The Kindly Ones*:

> [Such works] deliberately engineer a sense of crisis in readers, viewers or listeners by attacking the cognitive and cultural mechanisms that keep our understanding of the Holocaust at a safe distance from our understanding of ourselves.[26]

On the other hand, Holocaust impiety still cannot escape the logic of mattering. It is yet another manifestation of the ways in which the Nazis and the Holocaust are treated culturally and intellectually as something that allows us access to profound questions of existence and the nature of the modern world.

Ironically, the obsession with the Nazis can actually make naming the danger represented by those who genuinely are their heirs more, rather than less, difficult. In the wake of the outrage at the Trump administration's policy of child refugee separation in June 2018, a number of commentators argued that not only were Nazi comparisons legitimate, they required a special effort to acknowledge that, given the ubiquity of such comparisons in the past.[27] Indeed, Mike Godwin himself felt the need to tweet after the Charlottesville riot in August 2017: "By all means, compare these shitheads to Nazis. Again and again. I'm with you."[28] That Donald Trump found it difficult to condemn the rioters was a reminder that, whatever the problems are with ubiquitous Nazi comparisons, it is preferable to having no interest in the Nazi's contemporary heirs.

The Nazis Ruined Antisemitism

If the Nazis still matter so much today, then Jews too are condemned to mattering, as we have often been throughout history. We are by now inextricably linked to the whole period to the point where it is sometimes difficult to retain a sense of our separate existence. While this has ensured that the Holocaust is widely commemorated, it sometimes feels like it is "Jews" rather than actually existing Jews that are memorialised.

So the Nazis ruined antisemitism.

They ruined antisemitism for antisemites by raising the stakes, forcing them to consider whether they want every Jew in the world to be wiped out, depriving them of the lazy everyday pleasure of disdaining Jews.

They ruined antisemitism for anti-racists, by making today's incarnations of antisemitism difficult to spot in comparison to the Holocaust.

They ruined antisemitism for the Jews. They took something we thought we recognised and rendered it strange thereafter. They unmoored us, setting us adrift in a world where antisemitism is clouded in fog and any attempt to fight it condemns us to a bewildering hall of mirrors.

But the Nazis' ruination of what was once a familiar form of hatred is as nothing compared to the destruction wrought to antisemitism by the Jews themselves. It was us Jews who performed the final *coup de grâce* on the dying body of consensus antisemitism. We were the ones who, more than anyone else, precipitated the rise of selective anti/semitism.

CHAPTER THREE:

How the Jews Ruined Antisemitism

In April 2016, Ken Livingstone, former Mayor of London and long-time stalwart of the now-resurgent Labour Party left, stated in a radio interview that Hitler "was supporting Zionism [...] before he went mad and ended up killing six million Jews".[1] That comment, part of an intervention in the ongoing Labour Party antisemitism controversy, led to his suspension from the party and his eventual resignation in May 2018.

Livingstone's argument draws on a particular reading of the relationship between Zionism and the Nazis that highlights negotiations between the Zionist movement and the Nazi government to enable the emigration of Jews to Palestine (then under the British mandate).[2] The 1933 Haavara Agreement, which enabled approximately 60,000 Jews to flee to Palestine in return for ceding a portion of their assets to Germany, is presented as evidence of an intimate relationship between Zionists and Nazis.

It should not really need to be said that the attempt by some Zionists, before the Jewish state was founded, to save a portion of German Jewry did not in any sense constitute "collaboration".[3] Making an agreement with Zionists did not make Hitler a supporter of Zionism any more than the Nazi–Soviet pact made him a supporter of communism. In any case, the Haavara Agreement was controversial within the Zionist movement at the time, as were later deals to save small numbers of Jews.

The significance of these accusations is that they allow an impossible circle to be squared. The Nazis are the embodiment of evil. Ken Livingstone has drawn repeatedly on comparisons to the Nazis to intervene in multiple contentious political debates (Northern Ireland for example),[4] to the point where he has been extensively satirised for doing so.[5] At the same time as Livingstone relentlessly invokes the Nazis as an absolute evil, he is simultaneously an opponent of Zionism and a supporter of the Palestinian cause. And who is perpetrating crimes against the Palestinians? The kin of the very same people who were the Nazis' principle victims.

How is it that victims can become perpetrators? For Livingstone and others, these are two entirely separate categories of persons; to willingly switch from one to another is incomprehensible, a sign of catastrophic moral failure. So it has to be explained away by treating Zionists as separate to Jews, as perpetrators only, and hence categorisable alongside the Nazis. The Jews that were killed in the Holocaust were victims of two sets of perpetrators. The survivors and their descendants that embraced Zionism were either duped by the Zionists or were never really victims at all.

Circle squared. Job done. Simple.

Blessed Victims

Ken Livingstone is not alone in seeing the categories of victim and perpetrator as absolute. This distinction isn't even confined to the left. Victimhood has a kind of status today. There are obligations attached to it. There are lessons to be learned. There is some kind of purpose to it all.

This hasn't always been the case, for Jews or anyone else. Some strains of Zionism viewed the Jewish Diaspora as synonymous with weakness, passivity and victimhood — and not in a good way. In the early post-Holocaust period, that could lead to embarrassment at or even contempt for the victims of the slaughter. Tom Segev has shown that survivors were not always treated with much sympathy, and they found it difficult to speak of their horrific experiences in the emerging Israeli society.[6] Menachem Begin's revisionist Zionists campaigned vociferously against taking reparations from Germany. Veterans from the pre-state right-wing Zionist militia Lehi assassinated Rudolf Kasztner, a Hungarian–Jewish lawyer who had negotiated with Adolf Eichmann to allow a small number of Jews to leave for Switzerland. Zionist historiography preferred to focus on resistance to the Nazis rather than those who had "meekly" gone to the slaughter.

Segev argues that the place of the Holocaust in Israeli society began to transform following the abduction, trial and execution of Adolf Eichmann in 1962. Not only did the trial give survivors a prominent public voice that they had previously lacked, the actions of the state of Israel transformed it into an active agent in the redemption of Jewish passivity. Today, Israel treats the Holocaust, and the redemption of its victims, as foundational to its raison d'être. The solemn visit to Yad Vashem is a standard part of any foreign leader's itinerary in Israel.

So central is the Holocaust as a trope in Israeli political discourse, some politicians are tempted into a Livingstone-like revisionism of their own. In 2015, Benjamin Netanyahu claimed that it was the Grand Mufti of Jerusalem who, by convincing Hitler not to expel the Jews to Palestine, set the Nazis on the road to extermination as a final solution.[7] This argument (rejected by most historians) knits up Zionism into a trans-historical whole: in fighting the Palestinians, Zionism has always been fighting the Nazis, as the two are the same.

The tendency of Jews to see victimhood as something to either be ashamed of or explained away pseudo-historically, has not been confined to Zionists. In her famous report on the Eichmann trial, Hannah Arendt, whose relationship to Zionism was highly ambivalent, was scathing towards the *Judenrat*, the Nazi-appointed Jewish ghetto councils, for helping to facilitate the Holocaust.[8] The contemporary heirs to the non-Zionist non-Soviet socialist (Bundist) tradition also emphasise acts of armed resistance, such as the 1943 Warsaw ghetto uprising, in their accounts of the Holocaust. While Lenni Brenner's accusations of Zionist complicity with the Nazis are fringe even on the Jewish anti-Zionist left, Zionism is often seen to have been an impediment to putting up a stronger fight against the Nazis.

Even if today the place of the Holocaust in both Diaspora and Israeli Jewish life might have changed radically, contempt for Jewish passivity still persists. The ultimate Jew-on-Jew insult is to call someone a "kapo", a trusted concentration camp inmate with authority over other prisoners. For example, in 2016, David Friedman, who subsequently became Donald Trump's ambassador to Israel, called J Street, the US pro-two-state solution campaign group, "far worse than kapos".[9] But it is not just the Zionist right that taunts the Jewish left with kapo accusations. In June 2018, the non-Zionist Jewish cartoonist Eli Valley published a strip in *Jewish Currents* that concluded of Jews who enable the Trump administration's crimes that "Kapo doesn't begin to plumb the depths of their betrayal".[10]

What enrages those who use such insults is the departure of Jews from idealised models of an authentically Jewish response to persecution. When experiencing persecution or having experienced persecution, a real Jew leaves the Diaspora, a real Jew stays in the Diaspora, a real Jew fights back, a real Jew is a socialist, a real Jew supports Israel, a real Jew hates Israel.

These disputes do not occur in a vacuum. They are influenced by, and influence in turn, the gradual ramping up of the status that victimhood confers in the post-war period.

There is nothing new about seeing the experience of victimhood as, potentially at least, redemptive. Christianity (and, to an extent, Buddhism) is founded on a myth of redemptive passivity; Christ allowed himself to be sacrificed for the sake of humanity. While Christian history is hardly a story of passivity alone, it does ground a sense that victimhood can be good for the world and the victim. The suffering of the serf, or of the indigent poor, could be rationalised as a sign of their childlike simplicity, their innate grace. Indeed, so full of grace is the sufferer, that in some cases the removal of their suffering has been actively prevented (think of Mother Theresa's "hospitals" full of joyously suffering unmedicated untouchables).

It doesn't take much to transform redemptive passivity into redemptive agency. The experience of having suffered can ground a burning desire to actively change the world and one's place within it. That is just as true for those who have not directly experienced that victimhood but see themselves as redeeming those that have. Stories of Christians suffering under the Muslim yoke helped to recruit volunteers for the Crusades, stories of atrocities committed by Catholics or Protestants helped to stoke the religious wars that followed the Reformation.

In modernity, the redemption of victims has been central to more secular causes. The redemption of the Serbians who died in the Battle of Kosovo in 1389 at the hands of the Ottoman Muslims, for example, became a cornerstone of the project of modern Serbian nationhood. For Marx, the proletariat, suffering under the yoke of capitalist exploitation became the class that will catalyse the revolutionary praxis necessary to the achievement of full communism.

The ability and desire to speak of victimhood expanded further in the post-war period. Previously silenced groups began to speak of their experiences and to claim the political agency necessary to redeem their own and their ancestors' suffering. Colonised peoples, minority communities, women and LGBT people sought their place at the political table, insisting that they would no longer remain hidden. It is surely a positive development that we have reached the point in human history where we are able to speak of suffering, where we can refuse the shame of the oppressed and attempt to ensure that no one will experience it in the future. But, like everything else in human history, this development comes at a cost.

The profusion of voices attempting to speak of their victimhood makes for a crowded and confusing public sphere, particularly in an age where social media allows almost anyone to speak publicly. That can lead to a degree of "competition" to secure a hearing, which encourages a depiction of the suffering of one's own group as uniquely terrible. The attempt to turn suffering into political entitlement sometimes sets off a process of "competitive victimhood" that is as inevitable as it is sordid.[11] Some political claims on behalf of groups that have suffered can be difficult to reconcile. There is no consensus as to what the political implications of victimhood should be, even within groups that have experienced suffering. The sense of entitlement that victimhood creates is universal or becoming so, but entitlement to what? The perpetuation of memories of suffering can make the resolution of today's problems almost impossible. When what Wendy Brown calls "wounded attachments", memories of suffering, are placed at the heart of group identities, it can actually make addressing and overcoming the causes of that suffering much more difficult.[12] As David Rieff argues, sometimes there is a value to forgetting, but who today can ever forget given the endless performance of memory?[13]

Disappointing Victims

In the post-war period, the commemoration of the Holocaust became a central project of Jewish communities in the Diaspora and in Israel. This has not been simply an inward-facing communal endeavour, but an outward-facing one too. The opening of the United States Holocaust Memorial Museum on the Mall in Washington DC in 1993 is one striking example of this. The institutionalisation of Holocaust Memorial Days in many countries (for example in the UK from 2001) is another.

As the most prominent genocide in history, this memorialisation inevitably arouses frustration among groups whose sufferings are less widely recognised. In the UK, Holocaust Memorial Day has been dogged with criticism over not giving enough attention to other genocides (the Muslim Council of Britain boycotted it for some years), even though it does commemorate them to a degree. For those who are attempting to draw attention to other genocides and other forms of oppression, it can be hard to resist piggybacking on the Holocaust. The term "Holocaust" gets applied to everything from the abortion of pre-term foetuses to the killing of animals for food.

In theory this is not a zero-sum game. Drawing attention to the Ukrainian, Armenian or Roma genocides does not negate Jewish suffering in the Holocaust and, most of the time, that is not the intention of those who seek to do so. While Jews often get offended when anti-abortionists or animal-rights activists use the term "Holocaust", they are not, in and of themselves, rival campaigns. But a certain "envy" of the Holocaust may be unavoidable.[14] Scholars have explored the "secondary antisemitism" that emerged after the Holocaust, a complex mixture of deflected guilt and resentment.[15] Some memorialisation campaigns are indeed constructed to rival, and even negate, memorialisation of the Holocaust. In Eastern European countries such as Lithuania, where there was significant collaboration with the Nazis and national repression by the Soviets, there have been campaigns to put local suffering on a par with that of the Jews and even to rehabilitate some of those who collaborated with the Nazis.[16] The notion of "double genocide" (one of Jews, one of Lithuanians, Latvians, etc.) is, in part, aimed at downplaying the Jewish Holocaust.[17] Neo-Nazis and Holocaust deniers have also attempted to cast allied bombing campaigns against Germany (Dresden in particular) as being on a moral equivalence to or worse than Nazi atrocities.

Part of the rivalry stems from a perception that the Jews have managed to turn their tragedy into political gains — the creation and recognition of the state of Israel. Whether this is a correct perception is another matter. While the recognition by the United Nations of Israeli independence in 1948 owed something to sympathy with the Jewish cause, the Zionist movement did not always foreground the Holocaust in the case they made to the international community. Indeed, the Zionist movement was in a strong position to eventually gain statehood even before the war. It is certainly true though that later generations of Israeli politicians emphasised the Holocaust as a form of justification for at least the existence of the state and often specific actions it takes as well. That also goes for Jews in the Diaspora when they defend Israel. This has led some critics, such as Peter Novick or Norman Finkelstein, to accuse what the latter calls the "Holocaust industry", of using historic Jewish suffering to deflect criticism of Israel, trivialise anyone else's suffering, and elevate antisemitism above other forms of oppression.[18]

The accusation that Jews have used their victimhood to further their own ends raises the question of what the appropriate response to their victimhood should have been.

Other than in a few countries the Jewish condition is not what it was in 1938. While the pre-war Jewish populations of some countries contained substantial proportions of assimilated and privileged Jews, in the post-war period Jews in many Western countries experienced unprecedented upward mobility and unprecedented security.

Today, Jews in many societies appear, on the whole, to be materially privileged in a number of respects. In the US, a 2013 survey found that 58% of Jews were college graduates, compared to 29% in the general population.[19] The same survey also found that 25% of Jews had a household income exceeding $150,000, compared to 8% in the general population. In the UK, the 2001 census showed that Jews were 40% less likely to be classified as having "no qualifications" compared to the general population, and 80% more likely to have a higher-level qualification than the population at large.[20] Jews also appear to be more privileged than other minority groups. The 2011 census showed that, in England and Wales, 19% of Jews were in "Higher managerial, administrative and professional occupations", compared to 6% of Muslims and, 7% of Black British and 11% of Asian British.[21]

Of course, poverty and related forms of deprivation certainly exist within Jewish populations, particularly amongst Haredi (strictly orthodox) Jews.[22] There is no evidence, however, that deprivation in the Jewish community, even in the Haredi community, is directly related to discrimination other than in isolated cases. Indeed, in terms of the hatred that Jews face, one of the most striking aspects of the monitoring of antisemitism in the UK, US and many other countries is how far certain issues that appear frequently in the monitoring of other racisms are largely absent. Discrimination in the job market, access to housing and social services, differential outcomes in the education system, confrontations with immigration authorities — these are not, in the main, the principle manifestations of antisemitism in Western countries today.

Jews in Israel have also joined in this upward mobility. In the immediate aftermath of the War of Independence in 1948 and post-Naqba, the new state was economically weak and strategically insecure, with a population of less than 900,000, about 80% of whom were Jews. Today, Israel's population is approaching nine million — boosted over time by waves of immigration from the Diaspora and a high orthodox Jewish birthrate — of which around three quarters are Jewish. Israel is a nuclear-armed regional superpower, with a liberalised high-tech economy, and is considered a high-income country by the World Bank. It has deep pockets of depravation and inequality, including its Jewish as well as Palestinian citizens, but so do many other high-income countries.

Israel's place in the Jewish world has also been transformed during its lifetime. Israel is now home to just over half the world's Jews. Since Israel's founding, almost the entire Jewish population of some Diaspora countries have emigrated to the Jewish state (and, in some cases, to other Jewish population centres such as the US as well). Millennia-old Jewish communities in places such as Iraq and Syria have left, often due to persecution and expulsion following the birth of Israel. Following the collapse of the Soviet Union, over a million Jews emigrated from its constituent countries to Israel. A steady stream of Jews have also left for Israel from more secure Jewish populations, including the US and UK, driven by a commitment to Zionism.

Even when Diaspora Jews have no wish to become Israelis, support for the Jewish state has become normative across most Diaspora communities. In one survey, nearly 70% of American Jews reported to be somewhat or very emotionally attached to Israel (with much higher proportions amongst Jews who have some kind of affiliation with the organised Jewish community).[23] A 2015 survey of British Jews concluded:

> British Jews are strongly attached to Israel. The vast majority of our respondents support its right to exist as a Jewish state (90%), express pride in its cultural and scientific achievements (84%), see it as a vibrant and open democracy (78%) and say that it forms some part of their identity as Jews (93%).[24]

While support for the principle of Israel as a Jewish state, and a close identification with it, is normative for the majority of Jews in most Diaspora communities, there are nuances. For one thing, a significant proportion of the fast-growing Haredi community does not identify as Zionist and some sects are actively anti-Zionist (that doesn't stop them actually living in Israel though). Further, a proportion of Jews who support Israel's right to exist do not identify as Zionist. In the previously quoted survey, only 59% considered themselves to be Zionist. This is likely to be due to a combination of factors: an older generation who understands Zionism to mean a commitment to live in the Jewish state and a younger generation that are critical of the current nature of Israel, even if they support its continued existence.

While anti-Zionists who actively support the end of the Jewish state form a small minority in Diaspora communities, there is still considerable internal conflict in Jewish communities over the question of Israel.[25] While earlier generations often believed that Israel should always be publicly supported, that position no longer holds as much sway as it did. Studies of UK and US Jewry have shown a persistent liberalism in the socio-political views of Jews, evident in the continued majority support for the Democratic Party in America. This liberalism is increasingly out of step with the right-wing Israeli government. For example, the 2015 survey of British Jews suggested that 71% supported a two-state solution and 75% agreed that the expansion of West Bank settlements constituted an obstacle to peace. While levels of support for the current Israeli government appear somewhat higher in the US, just 38% of the 2013 US survey sample believed the Israeli government is making a sincere effort to make peace with the Palestinians.[26] In recent years there has been much debate amongst American Jewish social scientists as to whether younger and more liberal Jews are "distancing" themselves from Israel.[27] Liberal Zionist campaigners have argued that the American Jewish establishment is now out of step with the younger generation in its uncritical support for Israel.[28]

None of this internal debate about Israel's current political direction means that a significant proportion of the Diaspora Jewry is likely to join with the pro-Palestinian left at any point soon. Even the most liberal Zionists find it difficult if not impossible to accept the right of the return of Palestinian refugees or the abandonment of the Jewish right to return. The Palestinian history of terrorism against civilians and the disturbing radicalism of Hamas usually prove too much to stomach. Further, when liberal Zionists support organisations in Israel/Palestine that promote coexistence (such as the New Israel Fund), they are not only demonised from the Zionist right, they are also out of step with the mainstream of pro-Palestinian campaigning outside the region, which usually abhors attempts to "normalise" relations.

In any case, the public face of Jews in the world is often via their most prominent organisations and leaders. While there is no omnipotent "Jewish lobby" of antisemitic fantasy, there is certainly a well-resourced constellation of Diaspora Jewish-run organisations that devote themselves, in whole or in part, to advocating for Israel.[29] Some of them work in close collaboration with Israeli counterparts, including the Israeli government. While there is no unanimity amongst them as to what Israel's interests consist of, the most prominent voices are those that are least ambivalent in their support. On Israel and other issues impacting on Jewish life, many Diaspora Jewish communities can draw on deep, close relations with their governments, political parties and civil society institutions built up over decades. In this and the wider public sphere, Jews in the US, UK and many other countries are neither invisible nor alienated from public life.

It is therefore hard to see Jews as victims anymore. Jews are closely allied to and able to take advantage of significant sources of geopolitical power. Jews are now in a position to exert their agency in the world in a way scarcely imaginable just a few decades ago. The vertiginous gap between what Jews have been and what Jews are now complicates any absolute distinction between victim and perpetrator.

This gap means that, for a significant section of the left, Jews have been a terrible *disappointment.*

Incomprehensible Victims

How would Jews have responded to the Holocaust had they been authentic victims? Jews could have responded to the Holocaust with a self-sacrificing universalism that refused to draw any lessons from the disaster for themselves alone, only for the world as a whole. Jews could have renounced exclusive identities and turned their backs on power and inequality. The survivors of the Holocaust could have left the camps, merrily marched back to their almost Jew-free hometowns, embraced socialism and the fight for universal humanity. Jews could have reconstructed the decimated ranks of the Bund and other pre-war socialist groups and doubled-down on our previous humanitarianism. Jews in wealthy countries could have refused to enter the professions and abjured their place in the upwardly-mobile middle classes.

Well, some did. Jews have a long history of "identifying downward" in the modern world, even as they were moving upward.[30] Jews were as prominent in the post-war Western left as they were prior to that. Some Jews joined the ranks of the cadre in the Soviet-imposed regimes in Eastern Europe. Yet Stalin left no place for a revived Bund.

Many Jews were purged in the 1950s in the Soviet Union and in 1968 in Poland.

Most Jews simply kept on keeping on, putting their heads down and assimilating themselves into the post-war world, upward mobility and nationalism included. They rejected the gift of absolute victimhood they were given. They learned the wrong lessons. Jews sought to become part of the webs of capital and power that had oppressed them, albeit leavened with a veneer of liberalism. Jews — of all people![31] — have proved to have been unworthy of the blessing of the Holocaust. And then they have the temerity to still insist that it is still possible for them to be victims, to suffer, today.

Is this unfair? Would anyone be this crude? Perhaps no one would come out and call the Holocaust a blessing, but there is an insistent discourse on the left that treats the post-war Jewish embrace of worldly power as barely comprehensible. By choosing to support Israel, they are placed beyond the point of empathy, to a place of mystery.

When Jews become mysterious, some will fall back on ways of speaking of Jews that draw on older, antisemitic tropes. Those tropes are not alien imports into the contemporary left. There is a long, "indigenous" history of left-wing antisemitism that has, variously, associated Jews with capital, demanded their complete assimilation and, in the Soviet Union, singled out Jews for purging and persecution.[32] This history long precedes the state of Israel but, post-1948, opportunistically preferred to target "Zionists" rather than Jews. Scholars who investigate left antisemitism have shown how "classic" antisemitic tropes can be replicated on the left; including everything from stereotypes of Jews as wealthy swindlers, to *Der Stürmer*-like images of devilish Jews, to exposes of "The Rothschilds", even to Holocaust denial.[33]

The ability of the left to spot such tropes and attend to antisemitism varies considerably. There is certainly a history of tackling antisemitism within left movements in a concerted manner. The more extreme forms of antisemitism, such as Holocaust denial, are usually called out. At the same time, campaigning against antisemitism on the left can, in some instances, result in ostracisation from it, sometimes leading to its victims becoming disillusioned and moving towards other political positions.

Even when antisemitism on the left is recognised and opposed for what it is, it can be very difficult for some activists to accept the privileged nature of some Jewish victims of antisemitism. April Rosenblum's combative and influential pamphlet *The Past Didn't Go Anywhere: Making Resistance to Antisemitism Part of All Our Movements* asserts that "Antisemitism's job is making the ruling class invisible".[34] Antisemitism can certainly fulfil that function, but it can also be directed by oppressed peoples against Jews who are solidly within the ruling class. Rosenbaum's attempts throughout her pamphlet to make antisemitism today a form of oppression like others avoids discomforting questions over how to understand and oppose antisemitism against Jews who are privileged.

The danger of ignoring such issues is highlighted when some on the left argue that that antisemitism in the current political context is negated by the Jewish transition to oppressor. Only if Jews make a full-scale renunciation of and restitution for their complicity in Empire, can antisemitism become recognisable again (but then of course it may not exist at all). As the French–Algerian writer and activist Houria Bouteldja appeals to Jews worried about Holocaust denial (known in France as "*negationisme*"):

> If you really fear negationism, it is urgent to lay to rest these ideologies that glorify you as supreme victims and create hierarchies of horror. You must do justice to the Roma, the homosexuals, the Soviets, and the communists who died alongside your own people, and you must just as urgently recognize one of Nazism's origins: the trans-Atlantic slave trade and colonialism.[35]

When faced with this kind of refusal, Jews are often tempted into a counter-assertiveness that risks overstating the threats they face, and doubling-down on their defence of Zionism. This does nothing to challenge the problem of incomprehension. A more productive strategy would be to argue that the Jewish embrace of Zionism was *understandable,* regardless of whether or not it was desirable. For one thing, modern Zionism leverages not just an enduring Jewish theological attachment to Zion, it also draws on a near-continuous Jewish presence in what is now Israel/Palestine. Further, in an age when nationalisms were emerging throughout Europe and the rest of the world, it would have been extraordinary if Jews had not developed their own. In such a context, and faced with multiple traumas and genocide, the fact that Jews increasingly came to see their existential security as only being possible within their own nation state was inevitable.

Whether you agree or not with the choice Jews made to support the Zionist project, this choice was a comprehensible one. I am not arguing for some kind of quasi-psychological "understanding" that Jews sought to vent their humiliation and rage on their own victims. Zionism in its various forms comes down to more than just finding a new whipping boy; it offers a vision of a place for Jews in the world. That real people came between Zionists and their idealistic visions, and that these people suffered at their hands, is undoubtedly true. But to see the infliction of suffering on the Palestinians as the *purpose* of Zionism is to miss the point. And certainly, more subtly-minded intellectuals, such as Jacqueline Rose, are able to empathise with the desire for a homeland amongst those who built Zionism, without sharing that desire or validating what emerged as a result.[36] As Brian Klug has argued, Zionism is "janus-faced"; it emerged simultaneously out of a Jewish desire for emancipation and out of European imperialism.[37] It may be understandable that Zionists or anti-Zionists choose to see one face without acknowledging the other, but it represents a dangerous desire to reduce ambivalence and ambiguity at the expense of empathy with either Jews or Palestinians.

To comprehend the choices that Jews have made is also a first step towards challenging engrained assumptions about who true victims are how they act. Jews are not the only ones who are a disappointment to the left. The proletariat itself has rarely justified the hopes that the radical left put in it. The great innovation of Leninism was to recognise that the agency of the proletariat was so diffuse that it required leadership and direction from an elite vanguard. The failure of the proletariat to consistently put itself at the vanguard of revolutionary change meant that twentieth-century leftist theory became increasingly preoccupied with explaining that failure. From Gramsci, to the Frankfurt School, to Althusser, a major current of twentieth-century Marxist thought emphasised the stifling power of the capitalist system to crush any awareness that the world could be other than what it is. Simultaneously, as the Soviet experiment descended into sclerotic tyranny, it also became necessary to explain how a revolution so full of promise could have been betrayed.

But if the Western proletariat had been irredeemably seduced by the baubles offered by the ruling class, and the possibilities initially offered by the Russian revolution were looking increasingly misplaced, there were other parts of the world where subaltern revolutionary fervour might be found. The "new left" that emerged in the 1950s and 1960s was inspired by the multiple struggles for liberation from colonial rule that broke out in the post-war period and by other revolutionary movements outside the industrialised West. From Algeria to Vietnam, from Cuba to China, could the global struggle against imperialism could provide the redemption that the Western proletariat were rejecting?

There was — and is — a lot riding on this struggle. If these liberation movements failed, were co-opted or ossified, who else was there to turn to, given that the Western proletariat was usually a dead loss? This desperate hope has meant that it has been very difficult to face up to inconvenient realities of what these liberation movements really consisted of or turned into. Too often, the heroic liberation fighter became a repository for Western fantasies and desires. Those, like Sartre, who found hope in Maoism found it difficult or impossible to confront the atrocities of the Chinese Cultural Revolution. The undemocratic outcomes of revolutionary regimes in Cuba, Venezuela and Nicaragua are explained as the result of their continuing imperialist subversion. The kleptocracies that were born out of decolonialisation in Africa are received similarly, or in embarrassed silence. Desperately, selected Islamist movements are treated as if they are anti-imperialists with unfortunate rhetoric in the "red–green" alliances that were forged in the 2000s.[38] So strong are the hopes that there is precious little recognition that, while imperialism exists and must be opposed, those at the sharp end of revolutionary transformations are not simply the creatures of Western leftist fantasies.

Amidst this unstable dynamic of hope and disappointment, Israel–Palestine has become a central preoccupation for much of the left. This was not always the case — for many years the anti-Apartheid struggle took priority — but it had certainly come to be so by the outbreak of the second intifada in 2000.

As Joel Schalit has argued, so intense is the interest in Israel–Palestine that it becomes "a figure of speech" and "a metaphor for the world".[39] That lives are being lost, that Palestinians are being oppressed, does not on its own account for the centrality of Israel–Palestine in the imagination of much of the global left — there are too many other, and often much worse, examples of similar situations that are largely ignored. In fairness, as Israel defines itself as a democracy, it must expect to be judged to the standards of other democracies, rather than the standards of autocracies. Even here though, there are plenty of other democracies that perpetrate horrors greater or equal to those of Israel's.

The significance of Israel–Palestine is that it represents the point where disappointment meets hope. In the same small piece of the world, the heirs to the worst genocide of modern times have demonstrated their failure to learn its lessons and their victims have the opportunity to erase that failure, to show what victims really are and should be.

The Zionist and Palestinian causes have to be framed as categorically different for this hope to be upheld. Zionism must be treated as a species of chauvinist nationalism at best and straightforward imperialism at worst. The Palestinian cause must be treated as wholly different from nationalism. Somehow, Palestinian liberation must be understood as a yearning for an egalitarian state in which Jews and Palestinians would be equal, the chauvinistic qualities of the Palestinian struggle being purely transient and epiphenomenal (where they are recognised at all).

It is only by treating the Jewish embrace of national sovereignty as exceptional, as a pathological response to the Holocaust and previous persecution, that all kinds of disturbing questions can be kept at bay. If Zionism is comprehensible, if the Jewish experience is relatable, if victims can be perpetrators, what does that say about other peoples? Could the tendency of other national liberation movements to lead to their own forms of oppression be similarly routine? Could most victims be ill-cast in their redemptive role? And might Palestinians prove a similar disappointment when and if they achieve their own liberation?

My pointing out that national liberation movements often become new kinds of oppressors is not an argument against Palestinian liberation. Rather, it is an argument for seeing Palestinians and Jews as what they are — flawed human beings who can rarely bear the weight of expectation that they are expected to carry. By decoupling victimhood from redemption, by recognising that the line between victimhood and perpetration as frequently unclear, we can recover the humanity of Jews/Zionists/Israelis and Palestinians.

The case of the Palestinians demonstrates the perversity of the expectations that the non-Western oppressed are expected to carry by their Western supporters. On the one hand, little or nothing is expected from them today: suicide bombs directed at Israeli civilians and antisemitic rhetoric are sometimes seen as unfortunate, but they are largely treated as understandable. On the other hand, Palestinians are also expected to be standard bearers for the wider project of human liberation. Palestinians themselves are often bit-part players in their own story. In the UK, for example, they were never at the forefront of Palestinian solidarity movements until relatively recently. Even the preoccupation with Palestine in the Muslim world can engulf the Palestinians themselves under the weight of competing agendas.

In the work of the postcolonial theorists who supposedly inspire much of the political action in favour of the Palestinians, we find a much more realistic account of the humanity of those who suffer. For Frantz Fanon, to be colonised is not to automatically be a hero, but to be someone who must go through a strenuous process of reinvention.[40] Liberation is not simply a material act; it is a thoroughgoing attempt to see oneself in one's own terms, rather than through the prism of whiteness. Arguably, to be cast as the standard bearer of Western anti-imperialism is to fail to escape the yoke of white expectations. The implication of Fanon's work is that true liberation is a liberation into otherness, rather than into being a carrier of others' hopes.

There are also readings of Jewish tradition that draw attention to the difficulty of truly leaving behind victimhood. As Michael Waltzer has argued, the book of Exodus depicts leaving Egypt as only being the beginning of a painful process of liberation, one full of dangers and reverses.[41] While Waltzer uses this reading to ground a liberal wariness of revolution, it is also possible to conclude that while revolutionary change may be preferable to alternatives, it is rarely sufficient to achieve true liberation on its own.

The contingencies of political activism can leave little room for a consideration of the more troubling questions of what liberation requires, and the disturbing tendency for oppressed to become oppressor. The violence Fanon saw as a step towards the remaking of the wretched of the earth can become an end in and of itself. The strenuous attempts that Edward Said made to understand the Jewish condition can be abandoned in favour of stereotype and hate. And years spent in the trenches fighting for a cause intensifies the personal investment in the struggle to the extent that it can be hard to avoid seeing the world in zero-sum terms.

Ironically though, it is only through limiting expectations of what the oppressed should be that we can truly grasp the horrors of victimhood. If the colonised, the persecuted and the deprived are automatically cast as carriers of liberating insight, then we risk seeing the Holocaust, the Naqba and countless other forms of suffering as ultimately positive in some way. Perhaps we might forgive this tendency as a very human search for consolation, but too often the result is expectations that cannot be met. If Jews today can be seen as victims, then they are victims of this failure to accept that the long history of antisemitism did not turn us into anything other than human beings.

Victims of the Right

It may seem as though disappointment is a particularly left-wing response to today's Jews. Certainly, the post-war rapprochement between the political right and Jews is evidence that we have largely redeemed ourselves from our previous non-white otherness and radical history. Jewish upward mobility and the achievement, for some Jews at least, of white privilege is precious evidence of the ability of capitalism to respond to the aspirations of minority groups and provides a useful reproach to other minorities. Whereas Israel is the primary source of disconnection between the left and the Jews, it is the opposite on much of the right. With Israel's statist economy now liberalised, with its suspiciously obstinate and strongly-accented early leaders replaced by smooth-talkers with fluent English like Benjamin Netanyahu, and with its status on the frontline against the Islamist threat, what's not to like?

Yet sections of the right are as capable of putting particular peoples on pedestals as the left, and as susceptible to the disappointment that so often follows. Poor people who refuse to beatifically accept their fate have never been liked by Catholic conservatives. The noble Pashtuns who resisted the Soviets in Afghanistan the 1980s became a severe disappointment in the 1990s. Tame tyrants such as Saddam Hussein proved a let-down in the long-term.

There is a similar undercurrent of disquiet when Jews do not fulfil the roles they are assigned. Sections of the US evangelical Christian right give a redemptive role to Jews in their eschatological visions. With Israel playing a central role in the end times, "love" of the Jewish state is a central theme in Christian right politics. While some US Jewish organisations have returned the love, the political centre-of-gravity of American Jewry remains, for the moment, solidly liberal. That has led to frustration from the Trump administration when the majority of American Jewry refuses to support it, despite policies such as moving the US embassy to Jerusalem in 2018.[42]

Right-wing supporters of Israel can be as unabashed at telling Jews what antisemitism consists of and what Zionism means as left-wing supporters of the Palestinians. Left-of-centre Jewish-founded groups such as J Street (which campaigns against the occupation but still affirms Zionism), have been described as antisemitic and anti-Israel by right-wing non-Jewish supporters of Israel.[43] One common conservative talking point in the demonisation of the Hungarian–Jewish investor and philanthropist George Soros — which often includes antisemitic tropes — is the spurious accusation that he was a collaborator with the Nazis in Hungary during the Second World War.[44]

For now, the actions of Israel are enough compensation for the often-lukewarm relationship between Diaspora

Jews and the far-right. That situation may or may not continue, but should Israel adopt a more liberal direction (however unlikely at the moment), it is quite possible that a similar sense of betrayal that the far-left feels from the Jewish people could arise. This would also impact on Jewish liberals in the Diaspora if they are seen as supportive of a turn away from the right in Israel.

Jewish tendencies towards centrist liberalism are frustrating to both ends of the political spectrum. In the post-war period, liberalism was the best political bet for Jews to place. Centrist politics enabled Jews to enjoy the fruits of upward mobility while still allowing some level of commitment to and empathy towards the disadvantaged and the oppressed. Liberal Zionism would similarly reconcile the dual desires for a Jewish and a democratic state. In recent years though, not only has centrist politics been increasingly ineffective in achieving this reconciliation, it has not satisfied those on the right and left who are no longer content with its compromises. The result has been to leave many Jews stranded, politically incomprehensible and subject to selective anti/semitism.

Where Does This Leave the Jews?

Returning to that controversial space outside consensus antisemitism, the hotly contested question of whether the likes of Ken Livingston are "really" antisemitic, should give way to a much clearer conclusion: Those accused are invariably uncomprehending, baffled, enraged and flummoxed by certain kinds of Jews (often the majority of Jews). The perceived lack of fit between Jews and what their politics "should" be is a mystery that must be solved one way or another. And all too often the solution is to ram Jews into a narrative that rides roughshod over how Jews see themselves.

Jews today are caught between competing definitions of who we are and who we must be. We are not convenient. According to taste we are colonisers and liberators, belligerents and victims, a religion and a state. The post-war obsession with the Nazis has inevitably corralled Jews into a place of significance that flatters us but that we cannot ultimately bear. That significance turns Israel–Palestine into *the* struggle, an object of fascination, horror and support across the world. The world can pick and choose the Jewish state that it imagines: Israel as the symbol of Western oppression, the symbol of resistance to Islamic supremacy, the symbol of redemption, the symbol of irredeemable violence.

However much the world wants to settle on the image of the Jew of their choice, something always escapes control. Some or all of us refuse to be what is required of us, causing frustration and disappointment. And that means that we have inevitably ruined antisemitism too, building on the Nazi's sterling work in doing the same.

We ruined antisemitism for consensus antisemites by seeking to take control of our existence, by building up worldly power.

We ruined antisemitism for those who do not wish to be consensus antisemites by ceasing to be defensible.

We ruined antisemitism for Jews, by not taking the easy route, by refusing to be "Jews".

Given the now inescapable fact that Jews as an entirety cannot be assimilated into narratives about what antisemitism is, non-Jews are increasingly being selective: choosing the Jews they damn and the ones they save. And we are playing along, telling the world who the real Jews are, the Jews that are worth defending. This has not only contributed to the ruination of any kind of understanding that can encompass Jews as a whole, it has contributed to our own fragmentation as a people.

As I will argue in the next chapter, it is not only Jews that are subject to selective hate. Jews are in the vanguard of a process that is disfiguring anti-racism.

CHAPTER FOUR

The Chosen Ones

You see them everywhere that people protest in the name of Palestine. They are usually at the front of the demonstration, honoured guests, proudly displayed. They have beards, sidekicks and black hats. They carry banners proclaiming that "Zionism and Judaism are diametrically opposed". They wear Palestinian *keffiyehs*, conducted prayer vigils at Yasser Arafat's bedside, meet with Hamas and even attend a Holocaust denial conference in Tehran.

They are the true Jews.

They are the Neturei Karta, a Haredi, strictly orthodox sect with a few thousand members worldwide. They are vehemently anti-Zionist, believing the establishment of a Jewish state before the coming of the Messiah to be blasphemous. Such a view is not uncommon amongst the plurality of sects that make up the Haredi community. What is unique about them is their militancy, their very public, media-savvy stance and their enthusiasm for sharing platforms with the widest-possible cross-section of pro-Palestinian activists. This has led them to be shunned even by most other anti-Zionist sects, by all Jews who even remotely identify as Zionists and by some secular anti-Zionist Jews.

What the Neturei Karta have going for them is that they look unmistakably and authentically Jewish. I have written elsewhere of how the black-hatted, black-cloaked and bearded man is frequently treated as the image of the "real" Jew.[1] When Jews who look like that join with pro-Palestinian activists, they provide irresistible confirmation of what many of them long to be true: that Zionism is not really Jewish, that Jewish Zionists are inauthentic, that pro-Palestinian activity is not only not antisemitic, it is truly Jewish.

The Neturei Karta are the chosen ones — chosen not by God but by humans. They preen themselves in the light of those humans who have picked them. They are a prototype, not just for the good Jew, the real Jew, but for other minorities within minorities that are beginning to be chosen in the same way. By looking at how Jews became the selectively chosen ones we might be able to spot how this process is being repeated with other groups — and perhaps stop it in its tracks.

From Philosemitism to Anti/semitism

The Neturei Karta are not alone in providing this invaluable service. Secular anti-Zionist Jews are also prominent in pushing back accusations of left-wing antisemitism. Organisations such as Jewish Voice for Peace in the US and Jews for Justice for Palestinians in the UK, while they certainly do not deny that left-wing antisemitism exists, push back forcefully against accusations that Palestinian activism is mired in antisemitism. During the UK Labour Party antisemitism controversy, the group Jewish Voice for Labour was set up specifically to defend Corbyn and the Labour left against accusations of antisemitism.

It is not only on the left that Jews are in the vanguard of pushing back against allegations of antisemitism. In 2017, when Steve Bannon was still in the White House, Rabbi Shmuley Boteach ("America's rabbi" as he is affectionately known to himself) proudly had his photo taken with this enabler of alt-right antisemitism. In October 2018, the German racist party Alternative für Deutschland proudly announced the formation of a Jewish branch, with nineteen members.[2] In July 2018, the Hungarian prime minister Viktor Orbán, a right-wing populist who is regularly accused of antisemitism, was warmly welcomed to Israel by Benjamin Netanyahu. Indeed, in recent years, the Israeli government and its leaders have come to be valuable allies in playing down accusations of antisemitism. In the wake of the October 2018 Pittsburgh synagogue massacre, Diaspora Affairs Minister Naftali Bennett argued that accusations of antisemitism against the Trump administration were "unfair", in part because the president is such a good friend of Israel. Bennett was perfectly relaxed about dismissing the concerns of the (largely Democrat-supporting) Jewish population of the US at the normalisation of rhetoric about George Soros and "globalists"; after all, supporting Israel automatically makes you a friend of all Jews everywhere.[3]

In such incidents, the Jewish tendency to disagree profoundly on fundamental issues is visible to the world. As Israel–Palestine became an issue with such widespread interest, the "discovery" of this diversity has been extremely useful to participants on all sides of the conflict. If you don't like what some Jews are saying, you can always find another set — in fact, we will probably approach you.

As a hardcore, militant Jewish pluralist, I am certainly

not arguing for some illusory kind of Jewish unity. Rather, I wish to highlight a sometimes-intended sometimes-unintended consequence of the tendency for non-Jews to seek out the kind of Jew that speaks their language on antisemitism. When Jews speak of their diversity publicly, they may be heard as saying something like: "We Jews are not all the same, you do not have to pay attention to all Jews, just Jews like me, the only accusations of antisemitism that matter are the ones that I make — and I am not accusing you". Whether or not we intend to send this message, many non-Jews now assume that it is perfectly fine, even preferable, for non-Jews to be selective as to which Jews they listen to about antisemitism and much else.

This selectivity enables a dynamic in which non-Jews can simultaneously be what some Jews consider antisemitic and other Jews consider "philosemitic" (pro-Jewish), produces anti/semitism. These days, rejection of one set of Jews is usually accompanied by the embrace of another set. This allows some of the frustration and disappointment identified in the previous chapter to be explained and mitigated. If Jews have disappointed you, then there will usually be some Jews who will tell you that this is because they were not proper Jews. By endorsing the ways in which one kind of Jew understands antisemitism, the strangest hatred becomes comprehensible anew, saved from its Jewish ruination.

How Racism Became Selective

It isn't easy to relate to humanity as a whole and it is even harder to relate to sub-sets of humanity as a whole.

What does it mean to love Jews/Muslims/African-Americans/Bulgarians? And what does it mean to hate them? Doing so in the abstract is not so difficult. Antisemitism persisted in England and Spain even after Jews were expelled. Muslim immigrants are feared in some Eastern European countries that only have small numbers of them. Conversely, philosemitism on the US evangelical Christian right persists in areas where there are few or no Jews.

What happens when collective abstraction meets the messy reality of human difference? It is perfectly possible to be antisemitic even when knowing individually likeable Jews — they become the exceptions — just as it is possible for philosemitism to withstand knowledge of hateful Jews. Possible yes, but also more difficult. Hating all of one group can be as challenging as loving all of them.

In his infamous speech in Posen in 1943, Heinrich Himmler directly addressed the challenge of maintaining hate against Jews that would be consistent enough to enable genocide:

> It's one of those things it is easy to talk about — "The Jewish race is being exterminated", says one party member, "that's quite clear, it's in our program — elimination of the Jews, and we're doing it, exterminating them." And then they come, 80 million worthy Germans, and each one has his decent Jew. Of course the others are vermin, but this one is an A-1 Jew. Not one of all those who talk this way has witnessed it, not one of them has been through it. Most of you must know what it means when 100 corpses are lying side by side, or 500 or 1000. To have stuck it out and at the same time — apart

> from exceptions caused by human weakness — to have remained decent fellows, that is what has made us hard. This is a page of glory in our history which has never been written and is never to be.[4]

As Himmler recognised, the true task of the genocidaire is to resist the call of individual human relatedness, to see individuals as an undifferentiated mass of life-un-worthy-of-life. The hardness this requires may be too difficult for most, and it isn't even necessary. It's possible to oppress, to persecute and even to commit mass murder while still leaving space for a remnant, either because that remnant is worth keeping, or because tolerating them can salve one's conscience. That has been the dominant, although not exclusive, path that racism has taken in the post-war period, but it has roots that extend much further back.

"Total" racisms, that render everyone not like you as unworthy of respect or even life itself, remain marginal today. The wholesale damnation of the entirety of a particular group is relatively uncommon (although it is resurgent, particularly against Muslims). Much more common is a selective approach that targets a particular sub-section of a minority for opprobrium while affirming the eligibility of another sub-section for protection. This is selective anti/racism.

Selectivity may be driven by pragmatic considerations. Even when Jews have been despised and marginalised, they could sometimes be useful in filling economic niches; selected "court" Jews might even attain a degree of respect as representatives of their despised brethren. The Nazis chose to leave some Jews in relatively tolerable conditions for longer than others, according to local circumstances. In Poland, the ghettoisation and extermination of Jews began with the invasion in 1939. In Germany itself, the Nazis moved slower and more carefully; the wearing of the yellow star was initiated later than in Poland, some categories of part-Jews were left to just about survive until the end of the war. The Nazis relentlessly persecuted the Czechs and allied with the Slovaks. Of course, in the long term this pragmatism would probably have given way to ideological consistency, but in the short life of the Third Reich, a degree of selectivity helped to facilitate an easier path to genocide and racial dominance.

Even when racial thinking may render multiple groups of people as inferior, in practice certain groups are usually selected for particular hatred. Those groups that are selected may vary over time. While anti-Chinese racism in the West is by no means dead, it is nowhere near as ubiquitous or as virulent as it was over a century ago; when the Chinese immigrant population of London was associated with devilish opium-pushing and white slavery, when the Chinese indentured labourers that built the railways in the opening up of the US west were treated as virtually sub-human. Similarly, the rapid rise of Muslims in the hierarchy of Western folk devils is relatively recent, even if it sometimes draws on older racial stereotypes. Jews are, to a degree, exceptional in the enduring quality of hatred against them, although even here the prioritising of Muslims over Jews as targets in some sections of the far-right may reflect a more-or-less-genuine accommodation with at least some kinds of Jews.

Selectivity provides a helpful mode of escape from ideological contradictions and dilemmas. The modern nation state has often resorted to selectivity to get out of some tricky binds. In particular, selectivity made it possible to preserve older prejudices and hatreds in the context of a modernity that seemed to demand their rejection. That the emergence of modern notions of liberal citizenship and equality happened quickly in some countries such as France and the US, and more gradually elsewhere, raised an obvious question: how far were the rights of "man" extendable to all? Did a national community of citizens require uniformity amongst its members? And could Jews, with their separateness, their group identity and their trans-national connections, be assimilated into the nation? This "Jewish question" was a major preoccupation in many countries through the nineteenth and much of the twentieth centuries.

Part of the significance of the Jewish question is that the Jews were seen as the prime embodiment of problematic difference. The drive to create a homogeneous national community impacted on far more than Jews. In France, the aggressive imposition of a unified French identity with a unified language resulted in the enforced withering away of much of the distinctiveness of Basque, Breton and Occitan culture, for example. Yet Basques, Bretons and Occitan-speakers did not trigger the same anxieties, the same flood of publications and arguments, that Jews did. The French state may have demanded assimilation into the nation from everyone, but certain kinds of differences were selected as particularly problematic. This made it possible to inherit the pre-enlightenment hatred of antisemitism and recast it as enlightened universalism.

Empire provided another mechanism through which universalism could be reconciled with the desire to treat selected categories of humans as inferior. As the rights of democracy were extended in the "home" countries, so they remained highly restricted or non-existent in the colonies. Even long into the post-war period, as European states began recognising racism at home, the extension of democracy to the colonies was limited. In Hong Kong, it was only in the last few years preceding the British handover to China in 1997 that a fully representative democratic framework was permitted. Empire often provided a welcome release from the frustrations of democracy at home. Leopold II's creation of the Belgian Congo in the late-nineteenth century as his own personal fiefdom was notorious for its brutality and provided a treasured sanctuary for a monarch of a small country hemmed in by constitutional restrictions.[5]

Modern imperialism emphasised its "civilising" mission. Racial hierarchies and exploitation became recast as the paternalistic care of colonised people that were not yet "ready" for self-determination. At the same time, imperial powers selected individuals or groups who were more "advanced" and could be trusted with a measure of responsibility. Many of the intractable ethnic conflicts that followed decolonisation were the results of imperialist policies that privileged certain groups over others, such as the Tutsis over the Hutus in colonial Rwanda.

The United States provides a different model for those who struggle to retain beloved racial hierarchies within an equally beloved democratic polity. The contradiction between official equality and the existence of slavery in the

US could not be solved other than by civil war. The struggle in the US stands as a warning of the inability to assimilate officially-mandated racism in the liberal democratic nation-state. However, by developing sophisticated practices of selectivity after the Civil War, it became possible to ensure the exclusion, marginalisation and persecution of hated others whilst still retaining a sense of democratic virtue. One way of doing so has been to develop social policies that are couched in unimpeachably non-selective terms but that impact disproportionally on particular groups. No doubt many of those who were instrumental in ramping up the "war on drugs" and the rapid rise in the prison population that followed from the 1980s had no racist intent, but it was also deeply satisfying to those who were looking to justify their own distrust or hatred of African-Americans, whose communities were devastated in the process.

Another method of selectively embedding racism is to construct a kind of hierarchy of racial otherness, the higher levels of which are less rigidly policed than the lower. "Whiteness", as a modern category, has proved to be selectively inclusive. While an African-American can never be white, Italians, selected Hispanics and Jews can be.[6] In the US, the Aryan Brotherhood prison gang has had members of "mixed" (although never "pure-blood") Hispanic and Native American origin, but never black members. The ability of whiteness to include as well as exclude ensures that a robust coalition can be maintained against the absolute antithesis of blackness. Similarly, in apartheid South Africa, most Jews were included in the privileged white category, and the more limited privileges accorded to the "Indian" and "Coloured" categories helped to buttress the breadth of the coalition ranged against the "African" category.

Even in its more benign forms, the nation state is an intrinsically selective construction. The most thoroughgoing attempts at embedding anti-racism and multiculturalism into the nation can be undermined by the inevitable fact that not everyone can be a citizen. Anything other than an entirely open immigration policy will inevitably create selectivity in terms of who can be entitled to the protection of anti-racism. In some cases, anti-racist legislation and restrictions of immigration can run in tandem. In the UK, the 1962 and 1968 Commonwealth Immigrants Acts that restricted immigration from former British colonies were closely linked to the legislation of the 1964 and 1968 Race Relations Acts that outlawed some types of racial discrimination. One could read the message being given as, "while we don't want too many more people like you, we will endeavour to behave decently to those who are already here".

While at times the struggle to balance humane immigration policies and anti-racism has been carried out with a degree of compassion, there is an inevitable contradiction between the two. How can one distinguish between the Mexican or Bangladeshi immigrant to whom one must relate to as a fellow citizen, from the Mexican or Bangladeshi who is in the country illegally? Current policies that enjoin citizens to share responsibility for policing immigration, for example by requiring employers to check immigration status — what has been called "everyday bordering"[7] — further exacerbate the contradiction. It is difficult if not impossible to be permanently suspicious and at the same time to embrace anti-racist diversity.

Media-savvy and ideologically flexible far-right groups can leverage this implicit selectivity to cloak their racism in anti-racist rhetoric. Britain First, for example, presents itself as a non-racist attempt to preserve the British people from the dangers of immigration and Islamism:

> Britain First rejects racial hatred in all its forms.
> British ethnic minorities regularly attend our events and activities.
> Britain First opposes Islamic extremism and mass immigration because they are a danger to the British people.
> Britons from all backgrounds are welcome to join our struggle to put British people first.[8]

Injunctions to "integrate" into the national community, while they can include an anti-racist commitment to fight barriers to integration, often end up selecting and castigating those minorities that have done so less effectively. The corollary of this is the selection for praise of those "model minorities", whose impeccable integration stands as a reproach to those who are obstinately retaining their threatening otherness.

Model minorities are socio-economically successful, obey the law and do not agitate. In recent decades, Jews have often served in this role, as well as other minorities such as Korean-Americans. It is a role that some Jews have embraced with enthusiasm. In the 1980s, Britain's then Chief Rabbi, Immanuel Jakobovits, established warm relations with the Thatcher government, and was ennobled in 1988. Not only did he defend the government's agenda and the prime minister personally, he unabashedly upheld the British Jewish experience as an example for more recent immigrants to follow. When, in 1985, a Church of England commission, led by the liberally-minded Archbishop of Canterbury Robert Runcie, published a report critical of the government's devastating neglect of the impoverished inner cities, the Chief Rabbi stepped into the ring with his own pamphlet. Defending Thatcherite values of self-help and thrift, Jakobovits offered a reading of the history of British Jewish immigration that counselled patient endurance rather than agitation:

> Jews at the time were content to be patient and to wait and struggle for several generations to attain their social objectives, whereas we now lived in an impatient age demanding instant solutions [...] it may still be salutary to remind those presently enduring much hardship and despair that others have faced similar trials before them, and that self-reliant efforts and perseverance eventually pay off.[9]

This version of the British Jewish experience ignored the widespread radicalism of the first and second generations of Jewish immigrants. The selective historical memory of Jakobovits fed into a similar selectivity within the British political right. Jews are entrepreneurs, natural conservatives and loyal Brits; so different from those troublesome blacks. Thatcher — who also promoted a number of Jews to her cabinet — was one example of the widespread move towards philosemitism on the political right. It is, of course, a highly selective philosemitism, dependant on

Jews not just becoming supporters of right-wing agendas, but of forming their vanguard. The neo-conservatives that provided much of the intellectual heft in the second George Bush administration were largely Jewish. They helped cement the alliance between Christian fundamentalism and right-wing Jewish Zionism; an alliance that is re-affirmed by philosemitic Christian statements about their love of Jews and Israel. The widespread right-wing adoption of the concept of "Judeo–Christian civilisation" represents a replacement of Jews as the principle other to Christian civilisation with Muslims. Jews can also feed more liberal myths. The "successful" integration of Jews into the nation can be seen as proof of the nation's essential liberal tolerance. In that light, more recent "failures" of integration, particularly among Muslim immigrants, represent not failures of the majority but of the minority.[10]

While loving or admiring Jews should not in principle be problematic, it is almost always selective in practice.[11] Right-wing philosemitism usually selects Jews over other minorities as worthy of protection and consideration. In some cases, when philosemites protest against antisemitism, it may be the only anti-racist activity they undertake. For example, amongst the protestors against antisemitism in the Labour Party at a March 2018 demonstration in London's Parliament Square organised by Jewish communal bodies were Ian Paisley Jr and Norman Tebbitt. Paisley, whose Democratic Unionist Party has long been associated with the chauvinist elements of Protestant Unionism in Northern Ireland, faced criticism just days afterwards when he shared an Islamophobic tweet by Katie Hopkins.[12] The former Conservative MP Norman Tebbitt is well-known for his criticisms of immigration and distrust of immigrant loyalty to Britain. In September 2018, Prime Minister Theresa May made a high-profile speech to a Jewish charity in which she vowed to root out the "scourge of antisemitism".[13] May was instrumental in developing the "hostile environment" policy that sought to make life uncomfortable for illegal immigrants, ultimately resulting in the deportation of significant numbers of Afro-Caribbeans who were, in fact, legally British citizens.

Philosemites may also select a particular kind of Jew for their love and either ignore or damn the rest. A good example of this is the British writer Julie Burchill, whose enduring self-proclaimed philosemitism causes problems for her when she encounters the wrong sort of Jew. Jews, for her, and Jewish men in particular, had always been objects of fascination. Jews are the awe-inspiringly brilliant survivors of the Holocaust, the hunky men on Tel Aviv beach and the antithesis of hateful Islam. In her memoire *Unchosen*, she recounts what happened when she became interested in converting to Judaism.[14] She started attending services at a progressive Jewish synagogue in Brighton, where she lives. The rabbi of the synagogue, Elizabeth Tikvah Sarah, is a lesbian with a long track record of involvement in progressive causes, including Jewish–Muslim dialogue. Predictably, it was not a meeting of minds and her interest in conversion collapsed amidst a very public row.[15] That Burchill has not found another synagogue in which to convert is perhaps a recognition from her that to join the Jewish people would be to embrace a connection to those distasteful Jews that spoil the pristine image that constitutes her philosemitism.

Philosemitism and antisemitism are intimately connected: creating the confusing amalgam that is anti/semitism. They also stem from the same source, which Zygmunt Bauman, borrowing a term from the Polish critic Artur Sandauer, defined as "allosemitism":

> "Allosemitism" refers to the practice of setting the Jews apart as people radically different from all the others, needing separate concepts to describe and comprehend them and special treatment in all or most social intercourse [...] it does not unambiguously determine either hatred or love of Jews, but contains the seeds of both, and assures that whichever of the two appears is intense and extreme.[16]

Bauman describes allosemitism as "ambivalent" and the Jew as "ambivalence incarnate".[17] Jews do not and have never fully fitted. They attract feelings of attraction and repulsion, often simultaneously. Philosemitism and antisemitism are an attempt to resolve this ambivalence, but it never works perfectly. As I argued earlier in this book, the widespread sense that Jews matter has a long history. This is a burden to Jews, even when they are showered with philosemitic love.

Jews and Anti-Racism

It is easy to understand the benefits of anti/racism and anti/semitism to those who found it hard to adapt to the modern injunction to not be racist. Selectivity helped to ensure that the consensus over anti-racism became palatable to the point that it pervades even many deeply racist societies. Anti/racism provides a way of consoling oneself that, while you can't outwardly oppose universal rights in diverse societies, you can at least find more subtle ways of applying them conditionally, or not at all, to those you loath. Arguably, selective anti/racism is a modest improvement on more unabashed forms of racism.

But when self-defined anti-racists become selective in their anti-racism, what is their excuse?

Whatever the left might be, those on the left usually proclaim some form of universalism that not only affirms the equal worth of all human beings, but also actively strives to combat entrenched systems of power that treat some human beings as of lesser value than others. The same issues with universalism that gave rise to the "Jewish question" still apply to left-wing universalism. How far does the project of universal human liberation necessarily require a universal human subject? What kind of difference can be tolerated within this project? And what happens when particular groups of people identify themselves with particularistic, rather than universal identities?

One current in left-wing politics certainly leaves little space for the continued existence of Jewish or other identities beyond the revolution. In the immediate aftermath of the Russian revolution, the communist party set up special sections, *Yevsektsiya*, to draw in those Jews who were so far untouched by revolutionary fervour. Their aim though was not to develop a specifically Jewish form of Soviet identity, but to facilitate the total assimilation of Jews into the communist project, initially through persuasion but ultimately through force.

This kind of aggressive universalism is no longer the dominant current in leftist political practice. Indeed, part of the importance of the post-war new left was that, through its engagement with anti-imperialist struggles in colonial societies and anti-racist struggles in Western countries, it opened up space for the possibility of the preservation of human diversity within the project of human liberation.

Whatever level of difference the left can or cannot accommodate, the possibility of selectivity is ever-present. Inevitably, different kinds of ethno-religious groups will show different levels of enthusiasm for and convergence with the wider, universal project. That makes it easy to be drawn into a selective affinity with those groups that are easier to incorporate. As racists and antisemites play favourites with some minorities or sub-sections of minorities while abusing others, so anti-racists have often found it hard to avoid playing favourites in the same way.

The anti-racist left have their model minorities too, those who conform to their expectations of what minorities should be. A model minority must face, at the very least, significant structural disadvantage and preferably active prejudice. And the model response to that disadvantage and persecution needs to be resistance in some form. It is most helpful when oppression is so endemic that a minority is left with few other options but to wear its pariah identity with pride. That people of colour are often at the forefront of anti-racist struggles in the US, UK and some other countries, is a reflection both of the seriousness of the prejudice they face, and of the ease with which they can be incorporated as a model minority into the left.

Those minorities, or sub-sections of minorities, who

keep their heads down and concentrate on climbing the socio-economic ladder can be difficult to incorporate into anti-racist work, however much they may also face prejudice and structural disadvantage. In the UK, Chinese and Vietnamese immigrants, for example, have never been at the vanguard of anti-racist campaigns. Muslims have also been difficult to include as partners in anti-racist struggles until relatively recently. Once the political quietism of first-generation Muslim immigrants was succeeded by a new, more politically assertive generation — often "awakened" as a result of the Rushdie affair in the late 1980s — it became easier to see Muslim identities as, potentially at least, radical and anti-racist. Since the 9/11 attacks, the surveillance and persecution that Muslims have faced in the West offers a golden opportunity to hang on the coat tails of their resistance. That political Islam may ultimately have very little in common with left-wing politics as conventionally understood is often no barrier to the formation of "red–green" alliances.

For the left, Jews, or some Jews at least, were once a model minority. Jews were at the forefront of a variety of pre-war radical socialist and communist traditions. Eastern Europe's "revolutionary Yiddishland" was a productive milieu for socialist, communist and anarchist activism.[18] This revolutionary fervour was exported to the Jewish ghettoes of London, New York and much of the Diaspora. This is a history that is easy for radicals today to celebrate. However, at the time, the embrace of Jewish radicalism alternated with antisemitism on the revolutionary left. Ultimately, once Stalinism became the dominant trend on the revolutionary left, many of the distinctive traditions of the Jewish left withered away and, at times, were actively suppressed in the Soviet Union and elsewhere. Amongst those diverse traditions of the left was socialist Zionism, which is progressively being written out of the radical canon, an embarrassment, a contradiction in terms. But there is no getting around the fact that, in its early years at least, there was a widespread affinity for Israel across the left.

Just as Margaret Thatcher purred with pleasure when Immanuel Jakobovits rewrote the radicalism out of British Jewish history, so the UK's Jewish Socialist Group's constant reminders of the British pre-war non-Zionist Jewish radical past (and concomitant silencing of other Jewish political traditions) is catnip to the British left today. The obsession with remembering the 1936 Battle of Cable Street, at which the Jewish and non-Jewish left stood side-by-side to beat back the fascists from marching through the heart of the Jewish East End of London, is both a nostalgic reminder of lost, glorious era — when Jews *were* Jews — and a reproach to what Jews have subsequently become.

Those Jews who retain a commitment to the Jewish tradition of non-Zionist secular radicalism are, inevitably, the Jews that sections of the left are most comfortable engaging with today. In April 2018, Jeremy Corbyn attended a third night Passover *seder* meal run by the Jewish radical group Jewdas. The group combines nostalgia for the Bund, for Yiddish and the radicalism of the pre-war London East End, with a mischievous propensity to provoke. Corbyn's attendance was leaked and caused outrage in the right-wing press.[19] In and of itself, the *seder* was simply an expression of one strand of the diversity of British Jewry, and for a left-wing political figure to attend was hardly offensive. There is nothing essentially wrong with being particularly interested in one strand of Jewish life. The problem is when an affinity for one kind of Jew prevents one from establishing cordial relations with another kind. The mutual incomprehension that has been painfully visible on occasions when Corbyn has held meetings with bodies, such as the Jewish Board of Deputies, that have a better (although far from incontestable) claim to represent a larger proportion of British Jews, is a sign not of his inability to engage with Jews, but of his enthusiastic history of engaging with a certain type of Jew.

Jews are caught up in an implicit tension in anti-racist politics. Anti-racism can be part of a universal struggle for human liberation and it can be part of a particularistic struggle for the liberation for one particular group conducted by that group for its own benefit. This tension is often submerged. When groups that are subject to the most direct and severe prejudice and disadvantage join in with wider anti-racist coalitions, it benefits both the wider coalition and the individual groups within it — the universal and the particular. However, Jews today are strong enough to conduct their own anti-racist struggles outside of these wider coalitions, if they wish to or are compelled to. Can particularistic anti-racism still be seen as part of a universalist project? Sometimes, amidst controversies over antisemitism on the left, there seems to be a tacit assumption that because Jews are able to fight antisemitism without the assistance of the left, the prejudice they face cannot be seen as truly serious.

There is a long history of anti-racist solidarity between Jews and other minorities, but as Jews became more privileged in the post-war period, so the cracks in these coalitions began to show. In the US, the alliances of the civil rights era between African-Americans and Jews have been seriously eroded. As early as 1963, Norman Podhoretz's famous essay for *Commentary*, "My Negro Problem — And Ours", acknowledged the difficulties that some liberal-minded Jews had in relating to African-Americans and saw the increasing tendency of African-Americans to speak for themselves as a barrier to solidarity.[20] In 2018, *Commentary*, edited by Podhoretz's son and by now an unambiguously conservative publication, ran a special issue under the stark cover headline "African-Americans versus American Jews" that posed them as competitors and, at times, antisemites. There have been multiple flashpoints in this conflict — the 1991 riots in Crown Heights between African-Americans and Haredi Jews, the antisemitic rhetoric of Louis Farrakhan and the embrace of Palestinian solidarity in the Black Lives Matter movement — but what lies at the root of it all is the unavoidable fact that African-Americans and American Jews now occupy vastly different structural positions to each other and that racism impacts on both in very different ways.

When black US politicians such as Keith Ellison or André Carson are accused of tolerating antisemitism because of their relationships with Louis Farrakhan, it becomes painfully apparent that maintaining links with someone who has a significant support within the African-American constituency will inevitably come at the cost of suspicion from Jews. In February 2018, Tamika Mallory, national co-chair of the Women's March, was castigated by the Anti-Defamation League for attending a Nation of Islam event in which Farrakhan denounced Jews in explicitly antisemitic ways, including blaming Jews for chemically inducing homosexuality in black men. Mallory, while she did not endorse Farrakhan's comments, would not distance herself from the Nation of Islam. While this might be incomprehensible to many Jews, it is difficult for many African-Americans like Mallory to reject an organisation that is deeply embedded in African-American communities. An article by Adam Serwer in *The Atlantic* argued that rather than being a sign of condoning antisemitism, Mallory's position was the result of an impossible dilemma:

> From the perspective of her critics, Mallory's refusal to denounce Farrakhan or the Nation appears as a condemnable silence in the face of bigotry. For her supporters, Mallory's refusal to condemn the Nation shows an admirable loyalty towards people who guided her through an unfathomable loss.[21]

Above and beyond black–Jewish conflicts, Muslim–Jewish tension has today become the most intractable issue in impeding anti-racist solidarity. As Israel–Palestine became the focus of the world's fears and hopes, Muslims across the world have often seen Palestine as a symbol of their wider frustration, insecurity and, sometimes at least, persecution. It is also inevitable that both Muslims and Jews in the diaspora often see the other as a kind of representative of the Israeli or Palestinian threat to their existence. This conflation plays out differently amongst Muslims and Jews. Jews outside Israel–Palestine have not responded to Muslims and Palestinians in the diaspora with direct violence, but some at least have been enthusiastic proponents for discriminatory practices and Islamophobia. Muslims in the West rarely have the agency necessary to produce "official" antisemitism, but in some European countries, such as France, violence and other forms of everyday harassment directed against Jews has become widespread.[22]

Given that it is also true that in France and some of the other Western societies where Muslim antisemitism has become a serious issue are also countries where Muslims themselves face endemic structural disadvantages, anti-racist practice becomes much more complicated. It can be easy to retreat into a kind of determinism in which Muslim antisemitism — or, indeed, any other kind of racism practiced by disadvantaged groups — is merely an unfortunate reaction to a wider racism. While it may be true to say that antisemitism might provide some kind of outlet for those made bitter by the racism directed against them, that ignores both the history of distinct forms of Muslim antisemitism and is in any case no comfort to those Jews who are threatened by it.[23]

There is much to be gained from a careful, historically-grounded comparison between antisemitism and Islamophobia. As Ben Gidley and James Renton put it:

> Something about the Nazi Jewish enemy and the contemporary Western Muslim enemy demands complete surveillance — the power to see beneath the veil permanently and everywhere — an imperative that is not apparent with any other racialised enemy in history. To put it another way, few in the West speak

> or have spoken of the fanatical Gypsy, the protean menace of the Hindu, the world conspiracy of the Irish Catholic.[24]

At the same time, Gidley and Renton argue that we also have to appreciate the "sharp separation of antisemitism and Islamophobia as political categories in Western states, international institutions of power and global civil society".[25] Jews and Muslims occupy different positions in European societies and this means that their experiences of antisemitism and Islamophobia — while the two discourses may use similar rhetoric — will also differ. Muslims are sometimes treated as "the new Jews" — and sometimes understand themselves that way too.[26] Practices of control and surveillance that were once targeted at Jews are now focused on Muslims.[27] Many of the resurgent far-right movements in Europe and elsewhere target Muslims now rather than Jews, and some even claim to be philosemitic through their professed support for Israel. This sometimes leads anti-racists to prioritise the fight against Islamophobia over the fight against antisemitism, and even treating the latter as not just barely relevant, but as antithetical to anti-racism. Jews may be treated as having been "superseded" as the subjects of human liberation by Muslims and others who did not throw in their lot with empire.[28]

The end result of this kind of thinking can be that fighting antisemitism becomes regarded as an affirmation of other racisms. One stark example of this was the cover of the left-wing paper *The Word* that appeared a few days after the demonstration against antisemitism in the Labour Party held in Parliament Square in March 2018.[29] It showed on one side a picture of the demonstrators, together with images of Theresa May and Tony Blair, and on the other side a picture of impoverished African children together with photos of Jeremy Corbyn, Ken Livingstone and the activist Jackie Walker, with the banner asking "Which side are you on?" The side that demonstrates against antisemitism is the racist side.

It didn't have to be this way. The tensions between the struggles against different racisms and forms of prejudice and disadvantage have long been recognised. From the 1970s, black feminists started raising troubling questions over the ways in which white and black women, while connected by their femininity, did not share a common experience of racialisation. The concept of "intersectionality" — originally coined by Kimberlé Crenshaw in 1989 and subsequently developed by Patricia Hill Collins and others into a major field of research[30] — draws attention to the ways in which different forms of power "intersect" as related, rather than discrete, systems. The concept enables a complex understanding of the uncomfortable realities of power that mean that it is possible to be marginal and vulnerable in terms of one ascribed identity, while being privileged in another.

Intersectionality is not supposed to mean that different forms of oppression can simply added to one another — a black disabled women is not simply triply-oppressed compared to a doubly-oppressed black able-bodied women — nor that only the most oppressed are to be prioritised over all others. Indeed, intersectional theorists are often motivated by an explicit rejection of competitive victimhood:

> Intersectionality theory's most central and still controversial claim effectively combats the reductionist tendencies of the Oppression Olympics. The competition for the title "most oppressed" stagnates when everyone is revealed to have some form of privilege and political agency within a larger structure of stratification.[31]

Nonetheless, it is extremely difficult to translate a nuanced appreciation of intersectionality into a similarly nuanced form of political action. The Women's March in the US has faced continuous difficulties in balancing the competing needs and priorities of women of colour, Jewish Zionist women and non-Zionist Jewish women. The organisers, and those of similar progressive activist projects, have been accused of "abandoning" Jews by positioning themselves in opposition to certain Jewish organisations and agendas – and vice versa.[32] It is indeed difficult to build an inclusive space in which those who understand the nature and source of their oppression very differently can cooperate effectively. When agendas and commitments cannot be reconciled, who should "lose" and either leave the coalition or remain inside while stifling concerns? It is probably inevitable that in progressive coalition-building those who are more privileged might be asked to sacrifice more of themselves.

A sincere attempt to understand the cross-cutting networks of power can therefore curdle into a politics in which the experiences of those who are seen as too "privileged" are rendered trivial. This can lead to a kind of mimicry of the selectivity that is ever-present in contemporary racism. Those Jews in progressive coalitions who do not identify as

Zionist and do not feel tied to the Zionist Jewish community find intersectional spaces much more convivial.

Addressing privilege necessarily and rightly means causing discomfort to the powerful. But there is always a danger that the powerful may end up being subjected to the same selective consideration of their humanity from which they themselves have benefited. What ethical duties are owed to all, including the oppressor, the powerful, the privileged? Even the most thoroughgoing attempts to create a truly universalist politics can flounder on this question.

Judith Butler's *Frames of War: When is Life Grievable*, written in the wake of the war on terror and the invasion of Iraq, offers a moving and subtle argument in favour of a universal recognition of our mutual interconnectedness that allow us to face the precariousness of existence.[33] Butler highlights the ways in which Western powers render some lives as less worthy than others, as inherently less "grievable". Yet she tacitly assumes that the grievability of Western lives, or at least some Western lives, is always assured and does not itself need to be protected or nurtured. Undoubtedly, Butler would see her project as extending grievability to all, but when such ideas are turned into political action, the struggle sometimes changes into one of exchanging people from the category of grievable to ungrievable and vice versa. In her own activism, Butler has concentrated on fighting Western abuses of power and has found it very difficult to face the realities of power and abuse when it comes from inconvenient sources. Her characterisation of Hezbollah as part of the left, although subsequently clarified by her to not imply support, is an example of the difficulty in establishing a truly universal ethics that can spot sources of power even when they are ranged against other, perhaps greater, sources of power.[34]

The indifference of some sections of the left to those suffering at the hands of Assad in Syria, or in earlier years to those who suffered under the Khmer Rouge or the Bosnian Serbs, is a testament to the ease with which a universalist commitment to human liberation can easily turn into a selectivity every bit as pernicious as the more overt forms on the right. Anti-imperialism can turn into a "pseudo anti-imperialism", as Rohnini Hensman puts it, that only opposes selected forms of oppression by selected, usually Western-supported, parties.[35]

How Jews Lose

Jews have often been the ones who lose when left-wing politics turns selective. Increasingly, Jews need to renounce Israel and Zionism to be able to take a full part in progressive coalitions. In the US, some activists have argued for the exclusion of Zionists from demonstrations and other forms of protest, or at the very least for taking positions on Palestine regardless of whether that will effectively exclude Zionists.[36] To continue to identify as a Zionist, of even the most liberal variety, can mean that every other point of political agreement is rendered irrelevant. Coalition-building is, by definition, an activity that requires a certain tolerance for difference. That it should be Zionism that provides the limit case for this tolerance raises disturbing questions over just why it represents an insurmountable obstacle.

This exclusion can also mean that Jews who refuse to renounce Zionism are excluded protection from some forms of antisemitism. Only the antisemitism that comes from the same (far-right) sources as other forms of racism can be recognised or combatted. For the rest, antisemitic attacks such as those on Zionist Jews from Muslim minorities in Europe may be seen as regrettable but inevitable given Israel's actions. The existence of non-Zionist Jews helps to facilitate this dismissal. If some Jews are willing to renounce Israel and Zionism, then why can't all of them? The warm reception that the anti-Zionist left gives to Jews who take this political path acts as a rebuke to the rest — if you could be more like that, not only would you be more secure, we would stand alongside you in fighting the forms of white antisemitism that do continue to exist.

Jews who refuse to renounce Zionism can become angry and resentful at the ways in which non-Zionist Jews are treated as the only Jews who really count on the left. Non-Zionist Jews are often dismissed as "AsAJews" — Jews who only identify as Jewish in order to speak "as a Jew" against Israel and the Jewish people — and treated as pariahs by Jewish communities; dismissed as not really Jewish at all. Yet the usefulness of those who speak as a Jew is not confined to the left. When Jews speak as Jews for or against a particular political position, they can be heard by non-Jews as saying that they are the only Jews who matter, the repository of Jewish authenticity. At some point or other, most of us have been AsAJews, even when we didn't want to be.

Whatever Jews at different points on the religious/ ideological spectrum don't share, the tendency to collude in selective anti/semitism and anti/racism is depressingly ubiquitous throughout. We allow ourselves to be used; we make the selective game worth playing. We are happy to join with our non-Jewish partners, indemnify them from antisemitism, and attack other kinds of Jews who accuse them of the same. We perform the good Jew/bad Jew dance for the delectation of humanity.

We allow ourselves to be used as a stick to beat other minorities. We allow the struggle against antisemitism to be separated out from struggles against other racisms. We can be tone-deaf to intersectionality, fighting the antisemitism of marginalised Western Muslims as though it were the same as the antisemitism of the white majority. We can be blind to the connotations of singling out minority women of colour (Jackie Walker in the UK, Ilhan Omar and Linda Sarsour in the US) as antisemitic folk devils. And at the other end of the Jewish political spectrum we can collude in the message that other minorities can behave as they wish towards Jews, that their antisemitism will not count.

Selective anti/semitism intensifies conflicts between Jews. We use non-Jews (and are used in return by them) to tell other Jews that they are not "proper" Jews. We look for external validation for our different ways of being Jewish. It even leads us to rediscover our dormant Jewish identities in the service of others. As Jenny Manson, the co-chair of Jewish Voice for Labour, stated at a pro-Palestinian event in 2018: "I began to identify as a Jew in order to argue against the state of Israel and its conduct".[37]

One accusation that is regularly made of anti-Zionist Jews is that, through their anxiety and self-hatred, they are desperately looking for the approval of the Israel-hating world. If that is true at all — and certainly that is not how those Jews feel and they definitely don't present themselves as craven — then it must be true across the spectrum. Zionist Jews can be just as craven. When Jews make alliances with non-Jews in order to further their own agendas over antisemitism and Israel, they may well feel that they are in control of the process and that they are forging genuine partnerships, but the line between using and being used can be very narrow. Our attempts to get closer to sources of power, on the left, right or centre, leave us vulnerable, at risk of manipulation. We can be baited and switched; lured by promises of support for or opposition to Israel, or by assurances of action against antisemitism, and then used as fodder for a range of agendas that we might not otherwise approve of.

The accusations made by antisemites that Jews have inordinate power, that we control the world, should be turned on their head: we are controlled by all, *useful* to all, part of power-plays that have nothing intrinsically to do with us. This usefulness is not exactly new. As David Wertheim has argued, Jews have often been used to legitimate non-Jewish ideologies and forms of politics.[38] The existence of the Jews was, for example, useful for Christianity as a representation of the otherness that lies beyond the boundaries of the Christian faith. What is much more novel is the instrumentalisation of Jewish diversity: the recognition of the existence of different kinds of Jews as a form of legitimation for non-Jewish power.

In making ourselves useful, we Jews have empowered non-Jews to speak for Jews. Often, what Jews describe as antisemitism might better be described as allosemitism, in Bauman's terms — a desire to "fix" what Jews are. For example, Caryl Churchill's short play *Seven Jewish Children,* written in response to the 2009 Gaza war, provoked a furious response from Jewish organisations, accusing it of antisemitism.[39] The play features Jewish parents struggling over what to tell their children about Israel. One passage, in particular, was accused of being tantamount to blood libel: "Tell her I look at one of their children covered in blood and what do I feel? Tell her all I feel is happy it's not her." I don't myself see this as blood libel, nor do I see the rest of the play's dramatisation of the Jewish struggle to relate to Israel as antisemitic. What I do see it as is extraordinarily presumptuous in its desire to speak for Jews and to unveil our Jewish inner life to the world. It is hard to imagine Churchill doing this with any other ethno-religious group.

The day is surely coming when other minorities will allow themselves to be used as comprehensively as Jews are. The US political right has long made space for the occasional good African-American. There is always a Ben Carson or an Alan Keyes prominently placed in rallies for racist Republicans. It makes good strategic sense for the far-right to lionise those of their number who are conveniently "ethnic"; a Dinesh D'Souza or a Raheem Kaseem. We have seen efforts to differentiate "good" and "bad" Muslims in Western societies, albeit that the love shown to good ones is generally much more insipid than the adoration shown to good Jews.[40] And some Muslims are keen to be the good ones. In Ayaan Hirsi Ali's book *Heretic: Why Islam Needs a Reformation Now,* she distinguishes between "Mecca", "Medina" and "Modifying" Muslims — and the latter are the only good ones.[41] She herself has rejected Islam. She offers up Muslims to pick and choose from even as she has separated herself from their fate. No wonder she is so popular in conservative circles.

Yet religiously conservative Muslims could, in fact, be an indispensable resource for Western social conservative agendas. After all, not all of them have brown skins, they are not always racially distinct, they can be kind-of white. At some point, the right will finally twig that in sections of the Muslim population they have a natural ally, ripe for instrumental veneration.

Can the day be far off when the left and right "adopt" different sorts of Muslims, who will then play the good Muslim/bad Muslim game for the world's entertainment? Certainly, in the parcelling up of the Middle East into the Sunni camp, whose crimes are overlooked by much of the right, and the Shia, whose crimes are overlooked by much of the left, we are seeing a new kind of twisted imperialism emerge in which everyone can join in — even the anti-imperialists. Selectivity on the left is beginning to expand from the Jews to those inconvenient Muslims. Anti-Assad Syrians have been excluded from "anti-war" activism.[42] The smearing of the Syrian volunteer rescue group the White Helmets as al-Qaida or ISIS-linked Islamist extremists, shows that, when convenient, those on the left who have long complained of the demonisation of Islam are not above doing the same when defending good Muslims like Assad (and his good Russian and Iranian backers).[43]

How do we turn back this apparently unstoppable tide towards an ever-more selective anti/racism? A first step is to think more deeply about whom to listen to...

CHAPTER FIVE

Whom Should We Listen To Now?

One awful irony that emerges when those on the left who have been accused of antisemitism indignantly assert their non-racist intent, is that they would be unlikely to see this as a sufficient defence in other cases of racism. Indeed, a kind of reversal can take place, in which the accusation of antisemitism is the manifestation of power and the accused is the victim. David Hirsh has argued:

> Many antiracist people in our time have been educated to recognize the accusation of antisemitism, rather than the antisemitism itself, as the dirty trick. They hear it as an attempt to smear and silence people who criticize Israel. Today's antisemitism incorporates the notion that those who complain about antisemitism are the racists. It treats the opponents of antisemitism, not the antisemites, as the cynical ones; it treats opponents of antisemitism, not the antisemites, as the powerful ones.[1]

Hirsh has dubbed this counter-accusation "the Livingstone formulation", after Ken Livingstone's long history of responding to accusations of antisemitism with responses that the accusers are cynically attempting to silence him for his stance on Israel.

These counter-accusations are made being accused of antisemitism *hurts*; it is exasperating, maddening, a slur on one's integrity. In the midst of the controversy over the Women's March and its relationship to antisemites such as Louis Farrakhan, national organiser Linda Sarsour wrote a long and passionate letter taking issue with her accusers. Her counter-accusation was that, however much she has done to condemn antisemitism, her very identity means that she will be criticised for who she is:

> I was already being labelled an antisemite and by extension the Women's March. It's very clear to me what the underlying issue is — I am a bold, outspoken BDS supporting Palestinian Muslim American woman and the opposition's worst nightmare. They have tried every tactic at their disposal to undermine me, discredit me, vilify me but my roots are too deep and my work is too clear and they have not succeeded.[2]

For Israel-critical Jews, the pain at being accused of tolerating or empowering antisemitism hurts all the more. In her introduction to a collection put together by the US group Jewish Voice for Peace, Judith Butler argues:

> Those who accuse those who have criticisms of the State of Israel of antisemitism know that it will hurt Jewish critics of the State of Israel in an emotionally profound way. They know it will hurt because they also know that the Jewish critic of the State of Israel also loathes antisemitism, and so will loathe the identification with antisemitism with which they are charged. In other

> words, those who make use of the accusation for the purposes of suppressing criticism actually know that the person accused is not antisemitic, for otherwise the accusation could not hurt as it does. Indeed, it does not matter whether the accusation is true, because the accusation is meant to cause pain, to produce shame, and to reduce the accused to silence.[3]

Even if you feel that charges of antisemitism aimed at the left are baseless, there is no way of avoiding the fact that denial of antisemitic intent has long been a common feature of antisemitism. Jean-Paul Sartre described antisemitism as a "passion", but a passion that is often coyly expressed:

> It is first of all a passion. No doubt it can be set forth in the form of a theoretical proposition. The "moderate" anti-Semite is a courteous man who will tell you quietly: "Personally, I do not detest the Jews. I simply find it preferable, for various reasons, that they should play a lesser part in the activity of the nation." But a moment later, if you have gained his confidence, he will add with more abandon: "You see, there must be something about the Jews; they upset me physically".[4]

This reluctance to express that passion is a form of "bad faith", a failure to be authentic to oneself. But it is a weaponised, cynical form: "They delight in acting in bad faith, since they seek not to persuade by sound argument but to intimidate and disconcert".[5] An inescapable logic emerges in which accusations and counter-accusations spiral out of control in a struggle to determine what is really in the other's heart. Antisemitism controversies therefore become intensely personal. In our self-obsessed age, the dominance of a vulgarised Sartrean model of personal authenticity turns accusations of bad faith into an existential threat to the self.

Bad faith and cynicism are almost impossible to prove. I could certainly describe the expressions of heartache and fear that I routinely encounter these days in the UK Jewish community. I could even describe the sincerity of the hurt felt by some of those accused of antisemitism. But this is a game that neither I nor anyone else can possibly win. This is about *trust*. And in a world where different views exist, where politics is inevitable, we cannot avoid making judgements as to whom to trust. Whom should we listen to? Who gets the last word?

These are not just questions about antisemitism and racism, they go to the heart of what democracy means. Democracy is a way of managing disagreement so that even if you lose an argument, you do not lose everything; you retain your right to speak and the possibility of being heard in future. If a political party, an ethno-religious minority or any other of the plurality of groups that make up a democratic polity are told that what they say about an issue is somehow inauthentic and mendacious, then the implication is that they must be removed from the democratic public sphere into a purgatory of automatic distrust.

We can at least say this: For all the blanket accusations and counter-accusations of bad faith, conflicts over antisemitism rarely *look* like anyone is acting cynically. They are full of anger, outrage and hurt. Looking at people's reactions, it seems that for a Jew to be accused of fabricating concerns about antisemitism is as personally wounding as a self-defined anti-racist being accused of antisemitism. That doesn't mean that the expression of such hurt precludes the possibility of bad faith. What it does mean is that, however inconvenient it might be, we should assume good faith unless there is overwhelming evidence to the contrary. While a blanket indemnity against the bad faith of either the denier or accuser is unwise, it might be possible to adopt a blanket agnosticism on the character of people's soul. It would also help to lower the stakes so that judgements about antisemitism are treated as necessarily provisional, based on the best evidence available at the time. Everyone should be guaranteed a hearing; no one should be guaranteed the last word.

Are Jews Too Sensitive?

Starting from a position of deliberate uncertainty might make it possible to ask tricky and sensitive questions about whom to listen to on antisemitism. This means focusing attention on Jews — as anti-racism should always begin with a focus on its potential victims — but *which* Jews? Selective anti/semitism means listening to only one kind of Jews. So the question becomes how to abandon selectivity and how to manage the consequences of doing so.

Selectivity and the intra-minority diversity on which it feeds has rarely been acknowledged in anti-racist practice. Even the most far-sighted anti-racist principles can flounder when encountering the messy reality of an intra-minority disagreement.

In his 1999 enquiry into the failure of the police to successfully prosecute the murder of Afro-Caribbean teenager Stephen Lawrence, Sir William MacPherson suggested the following definition of a "racist incident":

> A racist incident is any incident which is perceived to be racist by the victim or any other person.[6]

This has become known as the "MacPherson Principle", and it is frequently invoked in the controversy over antisemitism in the Labour Party. For example, in summer 2018, the Labour Party's proposed amended definition of antisemitism (discussed in Chapter One) was accused of breaching this principle by not accepting the IHRA definition.[7] However the principle raises as many questions as it answers. While MacPherson's recommendations only implied that complaints of having been a victim of racism should be investigated as such by the police (in the same way that accusations of rape should be investigated as rapes, regardless of whether a prosecution and conviction is eventually achieved), even in that limited sense it does not really grapple with the ways in which members of minority groups may perceive racism very differently from each other. And, in any case, are there really no limits as to what should be taken seriously as a complaint of racism or antisemitism?

In December 2015 a controversial Israeli-born writer, Tuvia Tenenbom, was invited to the UK Limmud conference. Limmud is held every year with 2,500 Jews of all kinds — orthodox, progressive, secular, Zionist and non-Zionist, liberal and conservative — gathering for a four-day festival of Jewish learning. Tenenbom's trenchant and aggressive attacks on left-wing critics of Israel met a mixed response. I had invited him onto a panel I was organising at Limmud but for reasons unrelated to his views on Israel, I had to drop him. This became something of a minor cause célèbre amongst Jewish right-wing groups who accused Limmud of censoring right-wing voices. On social media, some went further. One tweet I received asked: "Since when did Limmud become an anti-Semitic gathering??? U people have no right to call yrselves Jews".[8] Given the evident absurdity of this allegation, would the MacPherson Principle really apply, should a formal complaint have been made to the Limmud or the hotel that hosted the conference?

It's tempting to respond to this problem by accepting that there will always be cranks who can safely be ignored. But who gets to define the cranks? And what is the maximal percentage of the Jewish population that can be treated as irrelevant? Organisations that claim (sometimes justifiably) to represent the majority of Jews have tried repeatedly to dismiss Jewish anti-Zionists in this way. Jewish minorities may be treated by the majority as marginal and irrelevant at best, as traitors and pariahs at worst. This only intensifies the selectivity that is endemic in responding to anti/semitism.

A better — if excruciatingly difficult — approach would be for Jewish groups, whether they are in a minority or majority, to insist that non-Jews should not listen to only one kind of Jew. In democracies, the majority should not erase the minority or treat it as though it does not exist. That said, it is certainly important to face up to the consequences of what will happen if you cleave to a minority

Jewish perspective on antisemitism or anything else. There might even be a pragmatic case to be made that, if you are incapable of weaning yourself from selective anti/semitism, it's better to be selectively anti/semitic in favour of most Jews rather than a small fraction.

Those Jewish organisations that represent the majority of Jews do not make it easy for those, particularly on the left, who do not instinctively relate to them. Bodies such as the Anti-Defamation League in the US or the Community Security Trust in the UK do not always look how anti-racist organisations are "supposed" to look. They are well-connected to police and other authorities, are well-resourced and have little interest in questions of structural disadvantage.

In our book *Turbulent Times: The British Jewish Community Today,* Ben Gidley and I argued that, by the 1990s, the official British Jewish communal leadership had undergone a significant historical shift in the way it communicated with both Jews and non-Jews. When Jews were a vulnerable, often impoverished minority, the more privileged leadership class of the community pursued a "strategy of security". They counselled Jews to feel secure in the country, to not rock the boat and to prove their commitment to Britain. They proclaimed to the non-Jewish population that Jews were securely loyal. This strategy was perhaps understandable in an officially monocultural country (although many Jews did rock the boat) but became anachronistic in a country that, from the 1960s onwards, publicly acknowledged its diversity and in which minorities became more willing to proclaim their discontent. So the Jewish communal leadership began in the 1990s to pursue a "strategy of insecurity", castigating Jews for being too secure, for intermarrying and assimilating, while eagerly complaining publicly about antisemitism. Ironically, the propensity of British Jews (and those in the US and some other countries) today to campaign publicly and vociferously on antisemitism is, in part at least, a function of the comfort and security that they enjoy.

This paradoxical self-confidence means that Jews in Britain, the US and some other Western countries can look as though they see danger everywhere. Survey findings show that Jewish perceptions of levels of antisemitism do not always coincide with the levels of antisemitism found in monitoring exercises and opinion surveys of non-Jews.[9]

Some might conclude from this that Jews enjoy the disproportionate attention they generate, that they overstate the limited racism they face and that they end up marginalising other, much more serious racism aimed at much more vulnerable minorities. This would be a mistaken conclusion. For one thing, the history of antisemitism teaches us is that security is never assured; after all, many of the Jews of pre-war Germany were wealthy and assimilated and this did not save them. Further, it is fairly perverse to condemn Jews for finally having the ability to take an aggressive stance on antisemitism. The corollary of this would be that only those whose struggle against racism and are doomed to fail could legitimately fight against racism.

Nonetheless, contemporary Jews may well have developed unrealistic expectations of the degree of security that they, or any other minority, can achieve. This is particularly true when it comes to Israel and Zionism.

Diaspora Jews did not always expect their countries to have close relations with Israel. Indeed, British Jews managed to cope with Zionist attacks on the British mandate forces in Palestine and the backlash against them that went along with it. As recently as the first Bush presidency, US–Israeli political relations were not always easy. Any diaspora will experience at least some tension between their commitments to the countries in which they live and the countries to which they are bound in other ways.

In the 1990s and 2000s though, Diaspora Jews became accustomed to generally untroubled relations between at least the US and UK governments and the state of Israel. Even when US and UK Jews were uncomfortable with Israeli actions, they knew that their governments had close enough contacts that they would be heard and given consideration. The fear that some UK Jews feel at the prospect of an avowedly pro-Palestinian UK prime minister (or even, for right-wing Jews, the reality of a mildly dovish US presidency in the shape of Barack Obama), shows how quickly one can get accustomed to a smooth experience of what is a fundamentally complex relationship. In America, Jews have become so used to a benign political environment for Israel that trenchant criticism becomes shocking to the point of panic. For example, Jimmy Carter's 2006 book *Palestine: Peace Not Apartheid* attracted a wave of condemnation from Jewish communal leaders and organisations, including insinuations that Carter was antisemitic.[10] The book's arguments, while strongly critical of the occupation, were in fact consistent with liberal Zionism. Its use of the term "apartheid" was intended as a warning of what Israel was becoming, not a blanket rejection of Zionism and Jewish sovereignty. But, from a former US president — even one who had brokered Israel's enduring peace with Egypt — this criticism was unhearable.

Part of the reason for this defensiveness is that Diaspora Jews have become used to using Israel and Zionism as a source of consensus, celebration and pride. In my book *Uncivil War*, I argued that, following the 1967 Six Day War, Jews in many Western countries used Israel as a way of bringing together an increasingly religiously divided community and as a focus for informal education for young people. While many strains of Zionism have been predicated on the negation of the Diaspora, in countries like the UK and US where Jews built a generally comfortable existence in the post-war period, a kind of "Popular Zionism" was born: one in which Jews came to feel obligated to have a relationship with Israel, but not necessarily to live there.[11] Israel became a "safe haven", a guarantor of Jewish Diaspora existence and a source of pride and self-confidence. Ironically, Zionism helped Jews feel comfortable in parts of the Diaspora.

Diaspora Zionism and Zionism as practiced by the state of Israel do not always align. The Zionism that aims for the negation of the Diaspora, for the immigration of every last Jew, may not be as dominant as it once was, but it is still a significant force. This can sometimes lead to a conflict of interest between Israel and the Diaspora when it comes to antisemitism. When Netanyahu or other Israeli leaders respond to antisemitic incidents in the Diaspora with a call for Jews to return "home", this suggests that there is no point in fighting antisemitism from anywhere but Israel.[12] Given that Israeli government's understanding of antisemitism may differ from that of some Diaspora Jews — developing warm relations with the populist right in counties such as Hungary despite the allegations of antisemitism that are levelled against them; fiercely opposing BDS even when Jews advocate it — it is not impossible that, in the future, we will see Diaspora Jews fleeing antisemitism being denied refuge in Israel, with the Israeli authorities treating them as implicated in antisemitism. The comfort and security that this form of Zionism provides is starting to become a highly conditional one.

Diaspora Zionism has also come to be predicated on a forgetting of the inescapably political character of Zionism. Liturgically, theologically and culturally, the Jewish connection to Zion is a constant theme throughout Jewish history. There has been a near-continuous Jewish presence in the biblical land of Israel that survived the destruction of the second temple in 70CE, and immigration to it is by no means purely a modern phenomenon. Nonetheless, the operationalisation of this connection into the project of building a modern nation state was not simply a matter of realising a centuries-old dream, but a calculated political act. The fact that Israel was built as a consequence of political — and hence, contestable — ideas and that the continued existence of the state does not erase that political character has become difficult to acknowledge. Zionism has become so deeply enmeshed in Jewish identity that it becomes very hard to hear any kind of critique of its existence. Amongst other consequences, this makes it difficult for many Jews to hear Palestinian narratives of the suffering they endured in the creation of the state of Israel. Even Jewish Zionists in the Diaspora who are more critical of Israel and the occupation have, until fairly recently, found it difficult to take a publicly political stance against the state.

One of the drivers of this forgetting of the political nature of Zionism has been the perception that the creation of Israel constituted a defence against antisemitism. A core assumption that Zionism makes is that, by having a state of their own, Jews will no longer be powerless in a world of great powers; even if they continue to reside in the Diaspora, Jews will always have a refuge and a place from which to fight back. When the Jewish right to a state is contested, many Jews will experience this as either a project to strip Jews of their defences against antisemitism, or as antisemitism in and of itself. When Palestinians contest the right of Israel to be a Jewish state — either peacefully or through violence — then they will be viewed as antisemitic by some Jews at least. The killing of Jewish Israelis by Palestinians, particularly the killing of civilians, can be experienced by some Jews as the latest link in a long, trans-historical chain of antisemitic violence. This perception is compounded by the fact that some Palestinians have, sometimes knowingly and sometimes not, embraced "traditional" antisemitic discourses and practices. For example, the 1988 Hamas Covenant endorses the *Protocols of the Elders of Zion* and accuses Jews of being behind Freemasonry and the Second World War.[13] It is also true that, regardless of the actions that Palestinians have taken, there is a strand of right-wing Zionist thinking that sees almost any kind of expression of Palestinian identity as antisemitic; as an "invented" Arab identity designed to prevent Jews from reclaiming the homeland from which they were exiled.[14]

However much Jewish views on Zionism and antisemitism might or might not be justifiable, they are frequently impractical. I have never encountered a Jewish supporter of Israel who argued that any criticism of Israel is always illegitimate (although I have encountered many who argue that Diaspora Jews should never criticise Israel in public). But the boundaries of what constitutes "legitimate" criticism are often very tightly drawn. Jewish complaints about criticism of Israel and Zionism often reflect unrealistic expectations about the degree to which others will go to accommodate their sensitivities. Pro-Palestinian activists are accused of "obsessional" and "disproportionate" criticism of Israel, and of "double-standards". There is often a great deal of truth in this. Many, although by no means all, pro-Palestinian activists have shown apathy or even support for atrocities carried out by Assad in Syria (some against Palestinian refugees). Yet when is political activism ever entirely consistent? Selectivity is endemic across the political spectrum and both defenders and opponents of Israel indulge in it. Without acknowledgement of that wider problem, Jewish complaints of disproportionate criticism of Israel can simply become special pleading — even when they are accurate.

While Jews are often reluctant to face the political character of Zionism, they are frequently accused of the opposite: cynically using antisemitism and Jewish identity as a way of accomplishing political goals in an underhand way. Some Jews and Jewish organisations have certainly used aggressive tactics to suppress particular kinds of criticism of Israel. One group, Canary Mission, has conducted covert and overt campaigns on US college campuses to target Jews and non-Jews who are critical of Israel.[15] Israel-critical Jews frequently attest to bullying and abuse from Jewish individuals and the Jewish community.[16] While direct accusations of antisemitism are not always part of this abuse, accusations of legitimating or permitting antisemitism frequently are.

Seeing such abuse as cynical ends up positing an idealised sense of "real" antisemitism unsullied by political machinations. Pointing out that accusations of antisemitism may be wielded for political ends tells us less than we might think. Not only is it inevitable that the political enemies of those accused of antisemitism will leverage those accusations, it would be astonishing if it were otherwise. Even when accusations of antisemitism are hypocritical, that is not, in and of itself, proof that those accusations are false. That antisemitism is an inescapably political issue does not mean that those who experience antisemitism are exclusively political actors, incapable of authentic feeling.

Accusations of antisemitism may sometimes be unfair or pursued out of ulterior motives and we cannot exclude the possibility that some accusers may have knowingly lied . Acknowledging this only means that antisemitism is a phenomenon that exists in the world humans have built, with all that that implies. Human beings can turn back and forth in a heartbeat between cynicism and idealism, truth and lies. What *is* antisemitic is treating this as a uniquely Jewish pathology. That is reason enough to default to an assumption of good faith when Jews make accusations of antisemitism. Or, at the very least, to do the hard work of research before accusing the accusers of bad faith.

Identity, Power And Privilege

We are where we are. The centrality of Israel and Zionism to the identities of the majority of Jews in the Diaspora is a fact. However much growing numbers of liberal and left-wing Zionists might be starting to take more critical positions on Israel, they are still likely to be unsettled when the very principle of Zionism is rejected, when it is seen as racist to the core, when its existence as a safe haven for Diaspora Jews is attacked. Unless couched in extremely sensitive language — something which, understandably, most Palestinians have little patience for and, more problematically, most Western pro-Palestinian activists are equally resistant to — head-on attacks on the legitimacy of Israel do not result in Jewish abandonment of Zionism, but its re-assertion. To a degree, anti-Zionism creates Zionists. Exceptional sensitivity is required if there is to be any chance that Jews will confront the political nature of Zionism and make space for critiques of it.

Jewish attachment to Israel is not a unique form of de-politicised identity. All kinds of ethno-religious groups treat political positions as non-negotiable, non-political facets of identity. Critiquing those positions as if they were simply political options like any other can be counter-productive. For example, when African Christian leaders treat opposition to homosexuality as fundamental to their religious identities, they know that Western attacks on this position will be experienced by many of their followers as a form of neo-imperialism. In such circumstances, those (often heroic) sections of these communities who are trying to resist may be treated as agents of outside forces, compounding their marginality.

To assert that there is a clear dividing line between political ideology and group identity is naive at best. As Dave Rich argues with regard to attempts to ban university Jewish societies in the UK for their support for Zionism:

> Those far-left activists pushing the anti-Zionist motions thought they were having just another political argument. For the majority of Jewish students, though, it was an attack on a fundamental part of their Jewishness.[17]

This stems from an enlightenment view of politics as a public activity generated by the private choices of free individuals. It treats the public sphere as entirely disconnected from religious and other identities that must be confined to the private sphere. The common anti-Zionist taunt that Jews are "only a religion" and therefore cannot claim national self-determination reflects a fundamentally modern, voluntarist Western view of what a Jew should be (a view that most anti-Zionists would be unlikely to hold with regard to other groups). Jews have often played along with this, modelling themselves on the modern Western concept of religion to be freely chosen like any other, but now they are being trapped in it too.[18]

Of course, group identities are neither fixed nor eternal. They do not contain an ahistorical "essence". Yet an anti-essentialist view of identity has also to recognise the fact that group identities often "feel" like they carry the weight of essence. As Kwame Anthony Appiah has beautifully put it:

> The fact that identities come without essences does not mean they come without entanglements [...] Identities without demand would be useless to us. Identities work only because, once they get their grip onto us, they command us, speaking to us as an inner voice; and because others, seeing who they think we are, call on us too.[19]

All of which leaves us with an appalling dilemma as to how to conduct politics when it impinges on closely-held group identities. The horrendous persecution that gay men and women are subjected to in some African countries requires action, but how to prevent the consolidation of the problem rather than its resolution? How might it be possible to support the struggles of women in Muslim countries without reinforcing Islamophobia? On the left, there is at least some awareness of the need to find a way to grapple with these issues. However, when it comes to Jewish Zionists, there is a limited recognition that the problem even exists. Overly simplistic notions of power make it difficult to understand the sensitivities of Jewish Zionists and others whose relationship with power is not straightforwardly one of victimhood.

There is certainly such a thing as power, and the structural disadvantages that flow from it. To be an African-American, a French Muslim or a resident of Somalia is usually to be at the sharp-end of repetitive and consistent forms of abuse, persecution, poverty and other forms of disadvantage, in subtle and not-so-subtle forms. To be a Jewish-American or a middle-class white Briton is usually — but not always — to face much more inconsistent forms of disadvantage at worst.

Yet the chasms that separate those on different sides of power structures can and do collapse at particular moments. At the moment a person is raped or assaulted, the structural resources that the perpetrator and victim can draw on become irrelevant. It may only be in moments of intimate assault that we can truly relate to each other as individuals, shorn of the structures that both chain and enable us. A white rape victim may, in some societies, have a better chance of receiving justice and support than a black rape victim, but that is only likely to mitigate the trauma to a degree. That Jews may have access to more effective ways of responding to racist attacks on them than other minorities does not wipe away the hurt that those attacks cause.

Globalisation, diaspora and immigration further complicate these already complex issues. Muslims may be a persecuted minority in some contexts and a persecuting majority in others. Similarly, while Jews in Israel and in the Diaspora may sometimes see themselves as a single people, global movements against Israel can impact very differently on Jews in the Jewish state and Jews in the Diaspora. As a wealthy, nuclear-armed, regional superpower, Israel has the agency to respond to Boycotts, Divestment and Sanctions (BDS) against Israel however it chooses. Whether or not BDS is justified or effective, boycotts are part of the armoury used by activists against states. Jews in the Diaspora have much less ability to withstand the blowback that a wider adoption of BDS would produce. For example, if Israeli-made products were to disappear from supermarket shelves, that would directly impact on the lives of Jews who keep kosher.

Power structures are not stable, no hierarchy is fixed for eternity. No one, however secure they may seem, can ever afford to believe that the wheel of fortune might not turn against them. Power and privilege are preserved so vigorously not simply to prevent a more equitable distribution, but also because of the fear that privilege, when challenged, might be "flipped" into disadvantage. Rulers can become the ruled. Radical political movements might aim for an egalitarian end of privilege for everyone, but as in the Soviet Union they often just end up reversing the system they oppose, creating a new elite to replace the old.

Too often, those who dismiss Jews as too privileged for antisemitism to be that serious are guilty of a deliberate ignorance of the ebb and flow of history. As consensus antisemitism in the US has grown and flourished during the Trump presidency — exemplified by the Pittsburgh synagogue massacre in October 2018 — so some of the relaxed attitudes to antisemitism from sections of the left have begun to look horribly premature. In February 2017, Michael Tracey, writing for the Young Turks media network smugly argued:

> [...] in general, anti-semitism remains a highly marginal force in American life. Where it does exist, it should no doubt be combatted. But inflating the threat doesn't do anyone any good. If it turns out, and is empirically demonstrated, that anti-semitism really is on the rise in the U.S. — is that cause for concern? Of course. But no such thing has been demonstrated, notwithstanding a handful of (contemptible and wrong) bomb threats.[20]

This habit of dismissing Jewish accusations of antisemitism can become so deeply rooted, that it extends even to minimising the antisemitism of one's supposed political opponents. Some of those who have been accused of antisemitism on the left do not simply deny that antisemitism exists on that part of the political spectrum, but downplay it more generally. The writer Alexander Cockburn, who was dogged with accusations of antisemitism through much of his career, wrote insouciantly in 2003:

> The encouraging fact is that despite the best efforts of the Southern Poverty Law Center to prove that the Nazis are about to march down Main Street, there's remarkably little anti-Semitism in the US, and none that I've ever been able to detect on the American left, which is of course amply stocked with Jews. It's comical to find people like Fox trudging all the way back to the 60s to dig up the necessary anti-Semitic jibe.[21]

Jews often think along a much longer historical durée and even in the most benign contexts may refuse to see Jewish security as a permanent state. The spectre of a world turned on its head is one of the reasons why even the most liberal Zionists mistrust demands by pro-Palestinian activists for a one-state solution and an end to the Jewish right of return. However much those who argue for this (particularly those who are not Palestinian) might talk of replacing Israel with a secular, binational state where there will be no ethno-religious privilege and where Palestinian refugees will be allowed to return, Zionist Jews often hear this as a demand for (counter-)ethnic cleansing or genocide, as a direct physical threat. Certainly, at least *some* Palestinian militants may want something like this, although that is usually not recognised by the Western left. All this means that, even when pro-Palestinian activism in the diaspora is framed in scrupulously non-antisemitic terms, even when it is entirely sincere in wanting an egalitarian post-national solution to the Israeli–Palestinian conflict, Jewish Zionists find it hard to hear this as anything other than a call for their erasure and for the cutting off of any escape route from Diaspora antisemitism.

Viewing the greater suffering of the Palestinians, it might be easy for those who are not Jewish and/or Zionists to dismiss these sensitivities as unwarranted at best. It would be better, though, to see it as something more understandable and, potentially, insightful. This stems from a very Jewish appreciation of the vulnerability that lies within the most apparently secure conditions of existence — what Judith Butler calls "precarity". This intense awareness of the precariousness of existence surely deserves a hearing. The reason to listen to even the most privileged Jews about antisemitism is that Jews have something valuable to teach about the endemic insecurity of a divided world.

Taking privileged Jews' experiences of antisemitism seriously is also a pre-requisite for relating to Jews who could not be described as privileged. It may be forgivable — if ignorant — to think that all Jews are privileged; the problem lies when the privileged are treated as beyond all consideration. This impacts on all Jews, not just the privileged. In 2006, Ilan Halimi, a young French Jew of Moroccan ancestry, was kidnapped, tortured and killed by an extortion gang, whose members were from a variety of African, Caribbean and Maghrebi backgrounds. They believed that Halimi was rich, given his Jewishness, and pressured his family to pay them large sums of money. In fact, Halimi was a mobile phone salesman from a modestly-off family. In this case, as with much of French antisemitism today, the assumption that Jews are too privileged to be respected ignores the similarity in circumstances between a significant proportion of Jews in France and other immigrant groups.

Too often, the left response to the consequences of the stereotype that all Jews are privileged is to point out the existence of Jewish diversity. In and of itself, this is an important project. Jews of colour and those from non-Ashkenazi backgrounds have begun to assert their non-whiteness, and to remind Jews and non-Jews of the multiracial nature of the Jewish people.[22] The problem is that the recognition of Jewish diversity can simply heighten selectivity. If the Halimi murder was a case of mistaken identification of Jews with white privilege, does that mean that the kidnapping, torture and murder of privileged white Jews is somehow excusable? In any case, non-white, non-privileged Jews do not necessarily draw the "right" lessons from their otherness. In Israel, Mizrachi Jews — that is, Jews from Middle Eastern backgrounds — have been a cornerstone of the electoral support for right-wing parties, driven in part by their alienation from the Ashkenazi establishment in the first decades of the state. And Halimi was buried in Israel — his family did not treat his death as an unfortunate blip in their solidarity with the non-white other.

Educating the world about Jewish diversity is an important project, but it will not save us from antisemitism.

It is the nature of antisemitism, like other racisms, to not distinguish between stereotype and reality, between majority and minority. To think of all Jews as privileged or, for that matter, to think of all Jews as any one thing, is to put even those Jews who do not conform to this characterisation in peril. So long as there is even one member of a hated group who does not fit the criteria for hatred, then hating all of that group will cause collateral damage to them too. If the fate of privileged Jews does not move you, if they are deserving of hatred, then you will inevitably end up colluding in the persecution of Jews who you might feel are undeserving of antisemitism. The fate of all Jews is bound together, whether they or anyone else likes it or not. By the simple act of identifying or being identified by the same label of "Jew", all of us are vulnerable to collateral damage when some of us are attacked.

Blaming the Victim

While Jews have been at the forefront of multiple political movements in modern times (the exception being fascism — although Jewish fascists have existed and continue to exist, they have never been in the vanguard), in the end Zionism, in its various forms, is what politically defines us today. Zionism, like other nationalisms, is a project that seeks to carve out a space in which a particular people can exercise agency, to determine their own future. However much that agency is constrained given our global interconnectedness, and however much Israeli governments and those who defend them often claim to "have no choice" but to act in a particular way, Israel is a powerful national state with a wide range of possibilities for how it acts in the world. Jews in many countries, including the UK and US, have well-organised and well-resourced forms of communal organisation and representation. The Jewish people are not without agency.

Given this agency, how far do Jews have some level of control over how and whether antisemitism is manifested? Is antisemitism today a response to the actions Jews take and, concomitantly, could a change in Jewish behaviour result in a change in the level of antisemitism?

This is an immensely sensitive area. I was reminded of just how sensitive it is when, in 2018, I made an offhand remark on a friend's Facebook post about a survey on antisemitism in the Former Soviet Union. The survey showed that Armenia had higher levels of antisemitic attitudes than any other FSU country. I commented "Well, I can't imagine that Israeli collusion with Turkish denials of the Armenian genocide helped matters". In response, I was called a "left-wing antisemite" and a range of other unpleasant things. There was a binary logic here: I appeared to be suggesting that Armenian antisemitism was provoked by Jewish behaviour. My opponents appeared to be implying that antisemitism is entirely disconnected from anything Jews actually do or are.

I regret my comment. While Israel's past collusion with Turkish genocide denialism disgusts me, as a sociologist I should have known better than attribute a monocausal explanation to a phenomenon like antisemitism.[23] In doing so I was indulging in a common tendency to see most antisemitism today as the inevitable blowback from Israeli actions. For example, an article in the *Morning Star* (subsequently deleted online), written in June 2018 in the wake of the killing of Gazan protestors in the "great march of return", argued:

> [...] surely the Jewish organisations and individuals who lately were protesting about growing anti-semitism in Britain must see that, as advocates of Israel's historical and still unremitting brutality against Palestinians, they will inevitably be regarded by some other British nationals as being indirectly complicit in that country's actions [...] no amount of protestations about the symptoms of rising anti-semitism or anti-Israel sentiment in Britain and elsewhere will end the problem until its root cause — Israel's criminal behaviour — is dealt with.[24]

Some have argued that this blowback is in a completely different category to antisemitism. Speaking of the assaults on Jews by French youth, often but not exclusively Muslim, from the deprived *banlieus*, Alain Badiou explains that "what these young people feel is not antisemitism, but rather a hostility, 'political but not well politicized', to what is perceived as the position of the Jews in France".[25] This is a hairs-breadth away from not just justification, but even encouragement. The corollary is that, were Israel to be "dealt with", the antisemitism it provokes (if indeed it could be called antisemitism) would simply melt away. In some formulations, antisemitism is held up almost as a kind of blackmail, something to be ignored until Zionism is shattered. As Lenni Brenner argued:

> When Zionism is politically defeated and all Palestinians have full equality in all the land between the Jordan and the Mediterranean, "Islamic anti-Semitism" will likewise lose its popular appeal. But not a minute before. Bluntly put: if you want to end today's "anti-Semitism" against Jews, end Zionism's "anti-Semitism" against Palestinians.[26]

This does at least acknowledge that the antisemitism "provoked" by Jewish support for Israel exists, albeit recast as something understandable and even logical. For those who argue that accusations of antisemitism on the left are confected or exaggerated, a similar mixture of acknowledgement and threat comes in the form of warnings that false accusations of antisemitism will end up producing real antisemitism. Sometimes this is expressed as a fear for the future. In July 2018, the British Jewish anti-Zionist Robert Cohen wrote:

> [...] what if Corbyn loses by a narrow margin? How will the millions who voted for him see the Jewish community and its three-year campaign to brand him toxic?
>
> The "Jewish War Against Corbyn" is not good Jewish communal politics. It's playing with fire.[27]

These kinds of explanations for antisemitism are unconvincing — to say the least — to Zionist Jews, and even some anti-Zionists may find them uncomfortable. Let us assume for a moment that antisemitism was purely a response to Jewish actions, either in Israel or elsewhere. Does that mean that, should Jews desist from those actions it would simply vanish? Hate has its own dynamic, and when cocooned in the framework of antisemitism, it becomes self-contained, independent of its initial causes. We know this from history. European antisemitism may have been stimulated in part by the belief that Jews killed Christ, but its continuing existence in secularising societies suggests that this "cause" ultimately became redundant. Indeed, systematic hatreds seek their confirmation, expanding to find new reasons to hate. Again, the history of antisemitism is not simply a history of endless repetition; innovations such as blood libels in the medieval period and "race science" in the nineteenth century ensured its continued vitality. The state of Israel did not burst into a world unsullied by Jew-hatred. Whatever anger the foundation of Israel and its subsequent actions may have caused, pre-existing histories of antisemitism, including within Islam and within the left, often gave form and substance to the outrage.

Yet if we reject mechanistic explanations, what is left? Sometimes, antisemitism is treated as a kind of virus that exists independently of what Jews do or do not do. Antisemitism, in this view, is based on the projection of fantasies onto Jews; fantasies that have no basis in reality. Israel is simply the latest excuse in a long line of them. The *telos* of this argument is that, given that antisemitism would exist regardless of the existence of Israel, better to have the state and face this enmity from a position of strength.

Hannah Arendt argued against the "fallacy" that antisemitism's choice of victims is arbitrary.[28] For her, antisemitic ideologies were based on antipathy towards what Jews really were (for example, bourgeois capitalists in some contexts). That Arendt argued that Jews had some "responsibility" for antisemitism did not mean that she thought that antisemitism was justified. In fact, her argument was as much as anything trying to actually explain antisemitism, because arguing that antisemitism is arbitrary explains precisely nothing. The best way of viewing Arendt's argument is as an injunction that we must put Jews — real, existing Jews — at the heart of any attempt to understand antisemitism. Beyond that, to talk of "responsibility", in however subtle a manner, is to risk so much hurt amongst the same real existing Jews, in such a way as to close down any possibility of communicating with them.

Between non-explanations that render the Jewish connection to antisemitism as entirely incidental, and explanations that see it as a consequence of Jewish behaviour, lies the ground on which antisemitism can be understood. Jews and non-Jews stand on this ground, intricately interconnected, as all of us are. Jews attempt to exercise their agency, subject to varying degrees of constraint, as does everyone else. Jews and antisemites exist in a relationship with each other, one that is bound up in all kinds of misapprehensions and fantasies. Amidst this tangle lies the secret of whether a Jewish change of behaviour could eliminate antisemitism, and how far there is a limit to what they could possibly do.

Somewhere between pure victimhood and total responsibility we might be able to unearth precisely what Jews could/should/must do. Somewhere in this continuum is Israel, Jews' relation to power, Jewish privilege. What we Jews do, what we build, what we believe, has consequences for others and how they see us. But even if we could finally pinpoint exactly where on the continuum victimhood and responsibility meet, what then? Where would we go from there?

Changing the Stakes

To even raise the issue of responsibility in conjunction with victimhood — of antisemitism or of any kind — is to risk compounding the wounds that antisemitism causes. How could I even intimate to a Jew who has been attacked on the street or abused online that they might never have suffered had we as Jews behaved differently? Even if it were true, would it not feel like a kick in the teeth? And this isn't just a Jewish matter. How, for example, is anyone who has been sexually abused supposed to react to discussions about responsibility?

The trouble is, to grant all self-identified victims a complete pass for all types of behaviour is also untenable. And if responsibility can ever only be with perpetrators, it risks the absurdity of seeing all victims as interchangeable: why do some people rape women and others bomb synagogues if women and Jews were not different classes of victims, attacked for different (albeit perhaps related) reasons?

The only way I can find round this impasse is to change the *stakes*. The reason this whole question is so hard is because so much rests on whether Jews or other classes of people can legitimately be understood as "worthy" victims. What if things were different? What if the acceptance of agency and responsibility could coexist with the acknowledgment of pain and suffering? This would mean taking a principled stance that certain kinds of behaviours — antisemitism, rape, abuse and so on — are wrong regardless of the behaviour of the victim. In and of itself, that isn't a novel argument. But its implications are rarely worked through to the point that I hope to do — to a place that is very uncomfortable.

Let's say that Jews really are over-sensitive cynics who act in bad faith to avoid being accountable for the justifiable hatred their behaviour provokes. Let's say that Israel is a state so piteously cruel and oppressive that its actions directly provoke hostility towards its Jewish supporters from people who would otherwise have never thought ill of them. Let's say that every single Jew is so callously privileged, so blind to the suffering they cause, that no accommodation can be made with them... *It should not matter!*

(And do I need to say that that is not what I believe about Jews? I hope not).

Antisemitism and racism, even in its selective variants, is a form of acting and speaking that is more than "just" criticism. It treats others not just as people with whom one disagrees on certain matters, but also as people who are somehow beyond consideration, beyond coexistence, beyond relationship. Everyone comes into contact with people whom one finds hateful from time to time. For the most part, the way we respond to them is to grit our teeth, maintain a façade of superficial politeness and minimise non-essential interaction. But if you have a co-worker you can't stand, you don't — or at least you shouldn't — subject them to violence, conduct campaigns against them, claim they cannot be part of democratic processes, create conspiracy theories about them and refuse to protect them against the abuse of others. You sit in meetings with them, you work together towards common goals, you even join them in a toast to Chris from accounting at his leaving drinks.

Again, let's assume that Jews, or a sub-set of Jews, are as hateful as they are painted. If you are to be a true anti-racist, you still have to treat them with some consideration, as you would an unpleasant co-worker. More than that: you have to protect them from others who would not treat them with the same consideration.

To be a true anti-racist you have to ask the question: How can we build a society in which privileged, oppressive, over-sensitive cynics can still enjoy the same level of protection as the good guys? And if you find that thought repellent or horrific, then good — because you should.

This is the ultimate answer to the antisemitism controversy: Not the embrace of some form of soggy liberal multiculturalism but the acceptance of something difficult and unpleasant. In the next chapters I will argue that, if we were to accept the unpleasantness of what living with diversity entails, if we were to acknowledge our suspicion and indifference towards each other, we might, paradoxically, be able to live together more harmoniously and be better anti-racists.

CHAPTER SIX

How To Cope With Diversity

In a sketch by the comedians Robert Webb and David Mitchell, "General Drayfox" (a supervillain clearly modelled on General Zod in *Superman II*) gloats from the roof of a London skyscraper at the city he has conquered: "Behold my wonderful new city in all its multicultural diversity!" Drayfox is nothing if not culturally sensitive. He taunts London's police chief who calls for the help of humanity's greatest hero and protector: "Who is this Captain Todger? And where is he or she, because of course captains can be male or female… Let him kneel before me! Unless of course he's an orthodox Jew and has an issue with kneeling for religious reasons in which case I'd be happy for him to pay his obeisance in whatever way he finds culturally appropriate". He is genuinely shocked to find that the foul-mouthed alcoholic superhero, Captain Todger, is in prison for statutory rape.[1]

Why wouldn't a supervillain, alien or otherwise, not combine a desire to take over the world with impeccable cultural sensitivity? And why wouldn't s/he also buy into the ubiquitous framing of diversity as a sign of the vitality of the modern city? While those who seek to dominate our (real) world have often leveraged many forms of sexual, racial and religious discrimination to buttress other sources of power, they don't have to do so. After all, what rapacious multinational doesn't have policies for equality in hiring procedures and against sexual harassment?

It isn't just that General Drayfox signs up to the language of diversity, he appears to take real delight in it. And why not? Multicultural and diverse London provides an endlessly stimulating environment, an inexhaustibly interesting panorama of tastes, smells, sights and sounds. This is what diversity has so often come to be mean: a buzzword, a synonym for a vibrant culture. It is something that we are encouraged to respect, even to celebrate. Diversity is a value that is upheld, with varying degrees of sincerity and superficiality, by a wide swathe of the right and the left.

But if you are celebrating diversity, you aren't really engaging in what it really means. Or to put it another way, if you're celebrating diversity, you are doing it wrong.

What Diversity Really Means

Diversity is not a pathological state. Diversity can be interesting, vital and invigorating. Yet it is also much else besides. The diversity of humanity isn't just exhibited in the ways we talk, cook, dance and sing, it is also manifested in beliefs, values, identities and practices that may be very difficult to reconcile with those of others. It is, of course, very easy to slide from recognising this into arguments that certain groups are "incompatible" with others. Islamophobia is often predicated on the argument that Muslim beliefs clash so profoundly with Western ones that it is impossible to mix the two in the same society without one side becoming dominated by the other.

This is NOT the argument that I am making. Aside from the essentialism that erases the diversity within both Islam and the "West", together with the long-standing history of an Islamic presence within the West, talk of defending "Western civilisation" against Islam can only ever end up creating oppressive societies that eventually target other kinds of difference. Further, there are strong reasons to welcome immigrants — Muslim and otherwise — into Western countries regardless of the challenges this may bring: post-colonial responsibilities, providing a haven for refugees, stimulating population growth in countries with low birth-rates, encouraging entrepreneurialism, bringing new skills, etc., etc. And in any case, climate change will create hundreds of millions of refugees that all humans will have a duty to find homes for.

I am not suggesting that diverse groups of humans should not live together, I am not even suggesting that immigrants have to "integrate" out the most jarring elements of their difference in order to make diversity work. What I am suggesting is that having diverse groups of humans living alongside you inevitably means living alongside people who will have visions of what it is to be human that are abhorrent to you. This is not simply a matter of religious, ethnic or cultural difference. Even countries with high degrees of ethnic homogeneity, such as Korea, have fought brutal civil wars within living memory. Modern nation states, democratic or otherwise, have often had enormous difficulties in enabling people who hold to mutually incompatible visions of human society to live together. When ethno-religious diversity is bound up with political diversity, when minority identities are also political identities, living together becomes even more of a challenge.

Too often, a full acknowledgement of the implications of this diversity has been suppressed. In earlier generations, immigrants into Western societies often "privatised" their difference. My grandmother's impeccable English accent was common to children of Jewish immigrants to the UK who, while they may have clung tightly to their Jewishness in private, had an overwhelming desire to "pass" as English in the public sphere and not replicate their parents' Yiddish cadences. Yet it is a mistake to think that, in an era of multiculturalism, a different kind of passing might not still be going on. Celebrating one's heritage in public can be an act of craven integration too. Immigrants may be expected to be colourful and bring from their lands of origins tempting new ethnic restaurants. On the left, they may be expected to play along with radical anti-racist practice. When Islamist groups adopt the language of the left and make alliances with radical groups, are they not "passing" too? Are they not playing down elements of who they are while they cavort for the delight of Western leftists?

Selective anti/racism has emerged in part because this passing cannot be completely successful. When Muslims perform for the pleasure of the left, they alienate the right. When different sorts of Jews play up to the differential expectations of the left and right, they alienate everyone in turn. And even when a minority, or minority of a minority, pleases those from the majority group to the extent that they will join them in anti-racist struggles, there is a disconcerting hidden bargain at work, as though anti-racism were a kind of reward for being politically simpatico.

All that said, in some respects the everyday capacity to live with diversity has proved to be much greater than those who warn of the corrosive effects of mass immigration have ever accounted for. For one thing, we should not ignore the long history of cosmopolitan cities and empires. Diverse societies are not new and, conversely, the notion that there are rigid barriers between "races" and ethnicities may be newer, or at least less historically normative, than is sometimes assumed. Even well into the modern period, mixing and intermarriage was not as uncommon in Western societies as it may later have become.[2] Today, as Paul Gilroy has argued, a "convivial culture" has grown up in cosmopolitan European cities; one that simply works:

> [...] there are other stories about "race" and racism to be told apart from the endless narrative of immigration as invasion and the melancholic blend of guilt, denial, laughter, and homogenizing violence that it has precipitated. Those emancipatory interruptions can perhaps be defined by a liberating sense of the banality of intermixture and the subversive ordinariness of this country's convivial cultures in which "race" is stripped of meaning and racism, as it fades, becomes only an aftereffect of long-gone imperial history rather than a sign of Europe's North American destiny.[3]

As Les Back and Shamser Sinha similarly argue, racism and conviviality co-exist, the latter subverting the former through the constant remaking of the multicultural by immigrants and minority groups.[4]

Such sociological perspectives draw attention to the ways in which individuals from diverse backgrounds can and do find ways to relate to each other convivially in everyday life. Nonetheless, this capacity to make diversity work is under increasing stress — to the point where everyday openness may be transforming into wary selectivity. Part of the reason for this is that, in cosmopolitan cities, the heterogeneity of the population has deepened to the extent that it is much more confusing to navigate. This is what has been called (controversially) "super-diversity", a process in which a relatively small number of substantial immigrant communities has given way to a multiplicity of smaller waves of immigration from a multiplicity of locations.[5] Whereas large waves of immigration from individual countries — such as Bangladeshis and Pakistanis to the UK in the post-war period — resulted in visible and identifiable communities that could and did become knowable and relatable, it becomes harder to place more recent arrivals from a wide variety of locations. There is no reason why it cannot be "normal" to encounter people from anywhere in the world in everyday life, but what happens when the background and the nature of newcomers is hard to parse? It is too easy to fall back onto selectivity, to treat British Asians, Afro-Caribbeans (and even Jews) as familiar and worth defending, and to ignore or be suspicious of the rest.

The difficulty in navigating this deepening diversity is exacerbated by the complexity of the web of diasporas that cross-cut our globalised world. There is nothing new about diaspora, but its nature is being transformed. Modern communication and transport mean that members of diasporas can travel and interact within them to a degree never possible before. At the same time, the tendency of minorities to play down their global interconnectedness (sometimes out of fear of being accused of having "dual loyalties") is eroding. This means that not only can some diasporas encompass being a vulnerable minority in one country and a dominant majority in another, their politics may simultaneously encompass minority anti-racism in one location and majority racism in another.

The process through which acceptance of diversity is under threat is paradoxical. Just as super-diversity threatens through confronting us with the unknown, other processes are also confronting us with a surfeit of knowledge.

Conviviality in complex societies requires a deliberate distancing to pull off. Richard Sennett has argued that "complex cooperation" requires a kind of silence and a propensity to not always speak one's mind.[6] By extension, I would argue that a strategic and knowing ignorance facilitates living with diversity. As Sennett says, "everyday diplomacy is a crafting of expressive social distance".[7] Conviviality requires a form of interaction that deliberately puts aside engaging with people's differing views of what it is to be human in favour of a mutual desire to live and cooperate together. But what happens when we are continually and forcibly exposed to the otherness that hides behind everyday interaction? What happens when we cannot easily come to terms with a broader realisation of who people are? The entanglement of political and minority identities forces us to confront such questions.

The possibility of strategically ignoring or remaining ignorant of unwanted information about the other has been progressively undermined in recent decades. As minorities abandoned quietist integration and asserted their right to speak for themselves and their concerns in the public sphere, so it became more difficult to ignore whether or not one agreed with the agendas they were pursuing. As we have seen, Jews have been particularly forceful in confronting the world with their uncongenial opinions on Israel and Zionism. But they are not the only ones. In the wake of the Rushdie affair, the increasing self-assertion of Muslim minority populations in Europe demonstrated not just their ideological diversity, but also raised troubling questions about free speech and censorship. All of this was, of course, a boon to racists, who were able to repackage race-based opposition to non-white minorities as ideological opposition to those who threatened freedom.

It is the Internet, and social media in particular, that has provided the final death blow to any possibility that the political diversity of minority populations could be ignored. In a world in which it is trivially easy to provide oneself with a platform to propagate one's views, it is extremely difficult not to confront the insistent self-assertion of the other. Even relatively homogeneous communities that once managed to reproduce themselves with limited internal conflict can be torn apart by the tendency of online arguments to spiral out of control. How much more difficult is it to maintain conviviality in societies that are highly diverse, ethnically, religiously and ideologically? Only by refusing online discourse altogether might it still be possible to remain ideologically opaque, to perpetuate the inscrutability that oils the wheels of everyday conviviality

We cannot claim ignorance anymore now that the views and agendas of others are trivially easy to discover. One of the defining features of most antisemitism controversies is the unearthing of a stream of "revelations" about the past alliances of those accused of antisemitism. Sebastian Gorka's activity within the Hungarian far-right or Jeremy Corbyn's platform-sharing with Islamists were not only easier to expose in an online age, the exposure itself received much more attention than might have been the case in the offline era. What might once have either been ignored or explained away as alliance-building based on a mutual decision to ignore the more problematic parts of the other's agenda becomes re-framed as unforgivable tolerance or naivety.

This leaves us with a dilemma though: Is our only choice between gullibility and paranoia? How do we build alliances, in opposition to racism and for other issues, in diverse societies where ideological divisions may be profound? How do we avoid endless fragmentation and disabling disputes? These are profound challenges that are too often dodged through resorting to selectivity. By judging some minorities harshly and judging others not at all it becomes possible to kid yourself that you are still embracing diversity, still practicing anti-racism.

Selectivity of this kind, while it builds on older forms, is a response to novel conditions. Diverse multicultural societies are not new; they have existed as long as agrarian societies have. Humans are perfectly capable of living in harmony with diverse others. What is novel is the confluence of ethno-religious minority diversity, the nexus of ethno-religious identity and politics, and online communication within democratic polities. Without even one of these elements, diversity would be — and has been — much easier to live with.

So celebrating diversity today is naive at best and dangerous at worst. To truly celebrate diversity would also mean celebrating those closely-held politics that are an integral part of at least some minority identities. It would mean celebrating liberalism, socialism, theocracy, fascism, Zionism, white racism, genital mutilation and much else besides. Who can possibly do that? When we celebrate diversity we are really only demonstrating our preference for certain slices of that diversity, for those groups and practices we find attractive. It's inevitable that we will be selectively drawn to some sorts of humans. But we shouldn't kid ourselves that that is the same as celebrating diversity. Selectivity is dangerous when it is framed as universalism.

That celebrating diversity is an impossibility is not a reason to reject anti-racism. Diversity is a challenge that we cannot avoid. Attempts to create homogeneity not only always fail, they are always oppressive. Anti-racism and the creation of alliances between groups are as important as they ever were. But we need to ground these struggles on a different kind of basis; one free from illusions about what diversity really means. To truly embrace diversity is to embrace the otherness of those whose way of life one might loath. And to truly be anti-racist is to fight for the absolute right of those loathed others to live free from abuse.

This agenda is excruciatingly difficult to pursue. It is, however, the best way for the left to respond to the rising challenge of those who would seek to roll back immigration and multiculturalism. Because anti-racists on the left have usually refused to face the ways that immigration can pose enormous political challenges, they have tacitly confirmed the assumption that it would be wrong if diversity was such a difficult thing to live with. A starting assumption that diversity is hard to live with provides a more enduring and resilient basis for fighting for immigration and multiculturalism.

Sullen Solidarity

The kind of anti-racist work that falls within peoples' comfort zones, that comes easy, is only the beginning of anti-racism. If you really don't want to be racist, you will have to do things that don't come easy, that are maybe even distasteful. That is a challenge that plays out differently across the political spectrum. It is difficult for liberals to feed in uncomfortable questions about power into their affirmations of anti-racism. It is difficult to for those on the right to recognise their responsibilities to those who are materially disadvantaged by racial hierarchies. It is difficult for those of the left to recognise the humanity of the privileged.

This last point has been one of my principle concerns in this book. How might it be possible to build a progressive politics that can concern itself with the wellbeing of — and, in particular, racism directed towards — individuals and groups who are, in some respects at least, privileged? This is an intensely frustrating question. It would seem to be, at best, a tiresome diversion of the "real" work of fighting for those who are most oppressed. However galling it might be though, it is much more important than it might initially seem. Because without some capacity to extend anti-racist work (or, indeed, other forms of progressive campaigning) to those "difficult" cases, the result will inevitably be the infiltration of the virus of selectivity into what should be a universalist political project.

There are enormous risks to a politics that aspires to this kind of universalism. It may simply reproduce the "third way" hypocrisies of the Blair and Clinton administrations, by failing to address power-differentials between minority groups under the guise of even-handedness. My contention, though, is that it is possible, provided that it is founded on a realistic and honest engagement with what diversity really means. The path from an anti-racist politics that selectively celebrates diversity to one that universally *accepts* it requires, above all, a change in attitude, to one of sullen, grim, forbearance. Anti-racism needs to become wary and never ever celebratory.

And therein will its idealism lie.

The most powerful kind of anti-racist solidarity is *sullen* solidarity. This is solidarity without illusions, without fantasies that those whom one defends necessarily have much in common with you. It includes defending political enemies and even those whom you would ideally like to become something else entirely. It involves, for example, anti-Zionists defending Jewish Zionists, conservative Christians defending Jewish secular radicals, and similar acts of solidarity that stick in the throat. Practitioners of sullen solidarity will fight for diversity to the last ditch, regardless of whom it encompasses. This is anti-racism as self-sacrifice, as an absolute commitment to fighting hate and abuse no matter how "deserving" its victims might be.

This sullen attitude can also enable the kind of progressive coalitions that are currently being torn apart through conflicts over antisemitism and other stumbling blocks to intersectional solidarity. If activists in the UK Labour Party, or in the Women's March in the US, were to see themselves as bound together not by bonds of empathy or even (God forbid) love, but as fellow disgusting human beings that are nonetheless necessary partners in bringing about a wider agenda, perhaps some of the current deadlock could be broken. Sullenly fighting with and for those vile Zionists might be the ultimate expression of anti-racist solidarity.

Solidarity with every type of human can lead to delusion or selectivity. Sullen solidarity though might be possible to extend universally. A cautious yet unconditional affirmation of one's shared connection to all humans — even, or especially, the loathsome ones — is robust enough to withstand what humanity can throw at it. If your expectations of humanity are limited, you are less vulnerable to corrosive disappointment. By being resistant to disappointment, you are not faced with the temptation to either turn a blind eye to others' crimes or to turn on them in anger.

Hating Ethically

The burdens of sullen solidarity are heavy indeed. Perhaps even more burdensome than showing solidarity to the loathsome is the restraining of one's instinctive attraction to some groups, cooling one's ardour for some causes over others. That is ultimately what a non-selective solidarity requires. However hard this may be, it may increase the chances of long-term success for progressive political projects such as Palestinian liberation.

Pro-Palestinian campaigners understandably try and demonstrate why Palestinian society and culture is worth fighting for. Yet to make the case for Palestinian liberation in terms of the excellence of their poetry, their heroic resilience and the worthiness of their political movements, is ultimately to weaken the Palestinian cause. The corollary of such arguments is that if the Palestinians were culturally uninteresting, hate-filled extremists they would be unworthy of liberation — which is, in fact, a common argument made by some defenders of Israel. Freedom from oppression must be absolute if it is to mean anything. Liberation is not a reward for good behaviour but a human right. For that reason, a more reserved attitude towards Palestinian society and culture may actually be a better basis from which to fight for Palestinian liberation. It also acts as a paradoxical guarantee to Palestinians: that they will not be abandoned when they become politically inconvenient (like Palestinians in Syria have been) and that if a future Palestinian state was to oppress certain kinds of people, they would not be forgotten.

It would be similarly productive and similarly counter-intuitive for pro-Palestinian activists to work on their relations with Jewish Zionists (and even Israelis) in the Diaspora and to engage seriously with questions of antisemitism. There is a tendency for Israel–Palestine to extend its borders, to become a struggle played out not just in Gaza but also in Paris or London. This makes the situation even more intractable and misses the opportunity to transform the Diaspora into a space for building relationships that could ultimately facilitate a just solution. It's a cop out to say that Jews in the Diaspora are not the same as Israelis or responsible for the actions of the Jewish state. Some Diaspora Jews do indeed see themselves as ambassadors for Israel. But it is in no one's interests for even the staunchest Diaspora Jewish defenders of Israel (as well as the growing Israeli Diaspora) to become engulfed in the ever-expanding conflagration. Taking Diaspora antisemitism seriously would ultimately serve the cause of Palestinian liberation, however much that may seem like a trivial distraction amongst those activists who burn with outrage at the injustices Palestinians are subjected to. After all, one of the responses by Jews to antisemitism in the Diaspora is to leave for Israel, which is hardly in the interests of Palestinians.

How can this possibly work? Even were pro-Palestinian readers to accept my arguments, they might point to the reality that people are drawn to this issue out of outrage and pain and the Palestinians' plight. Surely it is asking too much to expect idealistic activists to swallow all of that in favour of such calculated sullenness?

At one point I had intended to call this book *How to Hate a Jew (Without Being Antisemitic)*. I chickened out in the end, but the more I write the more I am convinced that this is the key to the problem. I am pessimistic that humans can let go of hate, anger and abusiveness. I am guardedly optimistic that it might be possible to develop an ethics of how, when and whether we give vent to our emotions. This is difficult to achieve within some belief systems. I once asked the former Archbishop of Canterbury Rowan Williams whether it was possible to hate ethically. His answer was clear: "From a Christian perspective — no".

Nonetheless, even for those who view hatred as incompatible with an ethical life, it might still be desirable to act so that the negative effects of one's hatred might be mitigated. And failing that it might be possible to *hate better*, to hate in such a way that one's political projects still had some chance of success.

The idea that there should be limits to hate is not novel. Laws of war existed long before the Geneva Convention. Part of their value lies not in abstract principles but in self-interest. It's simply a good idea to treat prisoners of war decently and to refrain from using certain kinds of weapons if your enemy does the same. After all, Nazi barbarity towards Soviet prisoners and civilians ended up being answered with similar abuses.

Peace can be made cynically, distrustfully and even hatefully. The 1977 peace treaty between Egypt and Israel never led to a rapprochement between the Egyptian and Israeli people; it only ushered in a "cold peace", in which collaboration is largely confined to mutually self-interested intelligence sharing and security collaboration. At a less extreme level, democratic systems also provide frameworks within which disagreement — and, sometimes at least, hatred — can be managed. While the Hobbesian view of the state as a way of preventing a descent into barbarity may be overly-pessimistic and barely-democratic by modern standards, it is still valuable as a way of thinking about how, while humans have not managed to abolish hate, they have managed to find ways in which it may be redirected and limited.

Some scholars of antisemitism have tried to find ways to make space for the possibility of something close to hatred towards Jews that would nonetheless not be antisemitic. Anthony Julius identifies a "rational" and "involuntary" enmity of Jews that derives from reciprocal conflicts with Jewish political projects; this is the category in which he places some Palestinian anti-Zionists.[8] For Julius, this enmity may or may not be just or fair, but it is different to the enmity of those who have "voluntarily" chosen the Palestinian side but have no other stake in their future, and different again to "irrational" enmities against imagined, non-existent Jewish projects (such as ruling the world or murdering Christian children). Rational enmity may sometimes be antisemitic but irrational enmity always is. While, unlike Julius, I don't believe that all forms of anti-Zionism are forms of enmity, he is surely correct to distinguish opposition to Jewish political projects that are part of the ebb and flow of political contestation, from those that are (consensually) antisemitic. Similarly, Gavin Langmuir has distinguished a "normal" form of being "anti-Jewish" from the pathology of antisemitism. The former is an inevitable part of inter-group conflict, whereas the latter is based on fantasies of what Jews are and are capable of.[9]

It is difficult to walk on the right side of the line between opposition to a Jewish political project and antisemitism, as the tendency of Jews to see such projects as part of their identities imperils this distinction from the outset. Nonetheless, the insight that protagonists in political conflicts need to somehow contain themselves remains crucial if there is to be any chance of creating an environment in which opposition to Zionism will not be experienced by Jews as antisemitism.

One way of containing conflict would be to reconceptualise anti-racist politics as the struggle for the right of minorities to be hateful. This would not be an anti-racism founded on any illusions about the lovability of the other — although it certainly would not exclude this possibility — but deliberately extend its practice to even the most loathsome. In some ways, this would be a paradoxical act of love: The fight for the freedom of the other to live without racist abuse should be a gesture that requires no reciprocity. Above all, this kind of anti-racism would not stand or fall on its ability to abolish hate, although that would certainly be a nice outcome; it would seek to abolish the expression of hate, however it is manifested.

The Radicalism of Restraint

An anti-racism that recognises the impossibility of abolishing hate would only work if it were founded on an arduous practice of *restraint*. Restraint is not a concept that is very fashionable these days. It connotes the stiff upper lip, the emotionally crippled, the love-starved child of an English colonial administrator at a draughty boarding school. Restraint is certainly a concept that can be wielded as a reproach to racial others — you are unrestrained, irrational, undisciplined quasi-children, unfit to govern yourselves; we are restrained, controlled, rational.

Up until recently, much of my politics and my writing has been founded on a rejection of such notions of restraint. I have been informed by feminist and post-colonial critiques of Apollonian white male subjectivity. I have learned much from Foucauldian deconstructions of the subtle and not-so-subtle workings of disciplinary power. I teach in a department of Psycho-Social Studies that is imbued with a radical psychoanalytic sensibility. Aesthetically, I revel in transgression and its libidinal tendencies; I celebrate extreme heavy metal's explorations in abjection.

In suggesting restraint as a necessary practice in diverse societies I am not turning my back on these traditions. Rather, I am trying to respond to what I consider to be the radically changed meaning of restraint in contemporary society. To be restrained in societies where there are limited or no possibilities for the expression of whole classes of experiences — particularly for certain classes of people — means something very different from restraint in societies where online technologies enable virtually unlimited self-expression. While acknowledging that the online playing field is not always level, it has nonetheless produced a vast space in which libidinous desires can be easily performed. In such a context, restraint — holding something back of oneself — *can* become a counter-cultural, even subversive, act. While acknowledging the emancipatory role that online culture sometimes has in allowing silenced voices to express themselves and join with others — #MeToo being one example — *not* saying what is on one's mind might also open up new political possibilities.

In any case, part of the reason why restraint has become neglected as a virtue is that it has been confused with repression. The popularisation of a vulgar Freudianism has propagated the assumption that if you are not speaking of something — particularly something difficult — you are necessarily repressing it. In doing so, this repression will undermine your mental health and you will "act out" in pathological ways. Yet provided that restraint is an aware, conscious and (at some level at least) voluntary act, then it need not be harmful, even if it might be extremely difficult. After all, psychoanalysis, in its classic formulations at least, never aimed at a world of boundless self-expression and a free-play of desire, merely at the possibility that we could come to some functional truce between Ego and Id. Of course, most of us do this successfully in parts of our everyday lives anyway. Why should this practice not be extended to difficult, painful issues such as the Jewish question?

Repression has certainly played a role in the antisemitism controversy. When overt antisemitism has been delegitimised, even consensus antisemites often feel compelled to deny antisemitic intent. How much more is this the case with selective anti/semites whose feelings about Jews are a confused knot of ambivalence? To acknowledge to yourself that you might hate or be exasperated by some Jews some of the time, would represent freedom from the strains of repression and the contorted self-justifications that it impels. Freedom from repression does not mean a compulsion to express that hatred. It can and should mean a compulsion to work towards voluntarily restraining its expression.

Minimal Civility

What would it be like to relate to people whom one might hate in such a restrained manner? How would this even work? By reviving another, often traduced concept — that of *civility* — we might be able to find a way through.

The concept of civility has had a bad press in some quarters, with good reason. It is difficult to escape its connotations of "civilisation" and the disparagement of the colonial other as an uncivilised being, in need of discipline, control and enslavement. For those who are descended from, or who advocate for, those peoples who have been marked as uncivilised, it can be hard to see injunctions to "be civil" as anything other than another attempt to silence and control them. Steven Salaita, an American academic of Palestinian descent, whose job offer from the University of Illinois was rescinded in 2014 after his angry tweets about Palestine came to light, has argued:

> In so far as "civil" is profoundly racialised and has a long history of demanding conformity to the ethos of imperialism and colonisation, I frequently choose incivility as a form of communication. (Or it is chosen for me.) This choice is both moral and rhetorical.[10]

As the horrors of the Trump administration unfolded, an ongoing debate developed over how far civility might restrict resistance to creeping fascism. Such small acts of resistance as refusing service at restaurants to Trump administration figures or the booing of Mike Pence at a theatre performance have provoked occasioned criticisms that they contributed to incivility in politics but also praise that this was no time to be civil.[11]

My own position is that civility does not need to mean being polite. It does not have to involve anything that smacks of smooth, urbane, agreeing-to-disagree. It should not imperil resistance. Rather, it rather be reframed as a self-interested, voluntary form of self-restraint; a calculated means of enabling a limited form of co-existence in diverse societies that will act as a firmer base from which political contestation can take place.

However, that reframing requires a substantial caveat. What I am interested in doing is reframing civility in cases of political controversy involving ethno-religious minority groups for whom particular forms of politics have become enmeshed in their ethno-religious identities. This means a form of civility that is fit for political conflicts over Israel, over religious fundamentalisms and related conflicts. I am unashamedly saying that, in these cases, politics requires "special" rules. In a diverse society, the default position towards ethno-religious minorities should be to work harder on civility towards them than one would normally do.

Part of my aim in advocating a specific form of civility for political conflicts that involve ethno-religious minorities is to enable a freer form of political debate. The enlightenment idea of a public sphere in which politics is conducted by free individuals unencumbered by any other ties is a chimera. Yet it remains an ideal to fight for. One of the reasons why Diaspora Jews hold so tightly onto Zionism is that criticism of it often produces in them a tremendous insecurity. If such political criticism were conducted more carefully, it might be possible for Jews to participate in such a way that they would be able to consider a wider range of political options. After all, there is a common tendency for Jews to defend Israel in public despite their misgivings because of the fear that to do otherwise will end up feeding antisemitism — and sometimes that fear is fully justified.

That said, members of ethno-religious minorities may need to become much more realistic about what they can expect to politically achieve within the societies in which they live. Certainly, Jews may have got too used to the hegemony of liberalism and liberal Zionism that proved so conducive to many in the post-war period. And even those minorities who have never achieved as much political influence as Jews will have to dial back their expectations. However much outrage and hurt members of Muslim minorities in Europe may feel at the publication of cartoons of Muhammed or other deliberate blasphemies, to expect a veto on matters of free speech is not a practical aspiration. But all these pills will perhaps be easier to swallow if the connection between politics and identities is recognised as something real and inescapable. When some Diaspora Jews feel fear and anger when their governments or political leaders do not support Israel in the way that they like, they might be able to tolerate such developments if their objections are not treated as a bad faith politicisation of identity.

It is not intrinsically racist to oppose the politics of a particular minority or section of a minority. What *is* racist is denying that such political identities exist; to refuse to recognise the ways in which Jews and others treat Zionism and other political projects as part of their very being. That doesn't mean accepting or supporting that politics; it means finding a form of civility that can somehow balance a recognition of the nexus of politics and identity with advocating an alternate politics.

The basis of this civility should be a pragmatic acknowledgement that certain others and their politics are not going to go away, that we are doomed to live alongside them into the indefinite future. This acknowledgement should self-interestedly accept that the only way to avoid falling into selective anti/racism is to find a way to interact with those minorities or sections of minorities that one doesn't much care for. It cultivates relationships with these others not because they are likeable, but because it is much less hassle to live in a society where members of different groups are not at each other's throats all the time.

Elsewhere I have called this "minimal civility".[12] That is, a form of interaction which avoids angry confrontation and seeks to engage with the hateful other in ways that do not pretend that politics can be separated from ethno-religious identity. In some instances, minimal civility may require that interaction be only conducted as perfunctorily as possible; in other instances, it may require painstaking effort to make arguments in careful ways. Minimal civility is guarded, exasperating to carry out and always restrained. It enables the sullen forms of solidarity that provide the alternative to selective anti/racism.

Civility is about more than just how we speak or do not speak to each other. All actions are communicative and, hence, civility takes us into the domain of policies and their enaction, as well as simply how these policies are spoken of. It is perfectly possible to be impeccably civil in speaking to and of Jews whilst pursuing policies that some Jews would consider antisemitic. Certainly, there are some who support BDS and/or a one-state solution in Israel–Palestine — both seen by many Jews as antisemitic — who are assiduous in avoiding antisemitic rhetoric and end up being surprised and hurt by the ferocity of Jewish anger at the policies they propagate. Extending minimal civility to the realm of policy cannot involve the acceptance of demands to exercise a veto. But it can involve a commitment to at least take into account the impact of policies on Jews or other minorities and to attempt to mitigate hurt where possible and practical. This is a commitment to embrace the inconvenience that the other represents, to make policy without illusions about their unintended cost.

Working towards minimal civility will also require equalising the nature of one's engagement with different sections of minorities by restraining love towards those sections of them to which you are attracted. How frustrating to have to be more civil towards those unpleasant Jews when there are so many pleasant Jews out there in whose approval you could bask! Minimal civility means resisting the appeals from sympathetic minorities or sections of minorities to pull you into their orbit and their factional conflicts. If we want to truly respect diversity, we have to keep a certain distance. While some minorities or sections of minorities plead for the love of the majority, giving this love will ultimately smother them.

The same is true for members of minority groups themselves. We also need to cultivate minimal civility towards those who would love-bomb us. This is the distasteful bargain: if we are to ensure that those who don't like at least some of us can manage to be minimally civil towards us, we have also to resist reciprocating the love of our "friends". In fact, in order to encourage a wider anti-racism, we may have to cultivate a wary distance, ceasing to encourage the idea that anyone could or should be a friend to an entire group of people.

What Do We Do with Our Anger?

Minimal civility cannot entirely solve controversies over antisemitism, nor the wider problem of selective anti/racism. Racism isn't simply a problem of incivility. It's also a problem of deep-seated attitudes, prejudices and hatreds. What minimal civility can do, if it were widely propagated, is to make racism a more difficult choice: something to be practiced by the committed and non-selective only.

Today, racism has become the easy option. Selectivity has allowed those who would define themselves as principled anti-racists to slide easily and unknowingly into the selective-racist abyss. Online communication has tempted many of us into easy, unrestrained expression of selective hate. All too often I have seen decent people casually drawing on some of the most ingrained antisemitic tropes without any thought. For example, a feminist academic of my acquaintance — someone whose work I have learned from, someone whose politics I largely share — once liked a fake news story on Facebook that "the Rothschilds" had been kicked out of Russia by Putin. When I pointed out the long history of the antisemitic Rothschild obsession, she seemed utterly bewildered that what had been the work of a second to express hostility to the banking industry could possibly have mired her in this swamp.

Minimal civility requires cultivating the restraint that leads us to think twice. The minimally civil recognise that communication is not something to be casual about. It is through learned practices of caution that minimal civility can survive its constant test — our human predisposition to anger.

Anger can turn difficult tensions into ones that are impossible to solve. Anger leads us to speak without thought, to cease to monitor ourselves. One example of this occurred in November 2018, when Linda Sarsour, national organiser of the Women's March, responded to criticisms from the Anti-Defamation League of newly elected congresswoman Ilhan Omar, who supports BDS. Sarsour claimed that attacks on Omar were "not only coming from the right-wing but some folks who masquerade as progressives but always choose their allegiance to Israel over their commitment to democracy and free speech". This accusation echoed the common antisemitic charge of "dual loyalty"; that Jews are compromised in their citizenship through their global solidarity with other Jews with Israel. As a Palestinian-American, Sarsour should have known, and probably did know, what it means to accuse someone of not being committed to their own country, and she has shown herself on other occasions to be someone who takes antisemitism seriously. But in the midst of a bitter dispute, she resorted to language that she might not have used in calmer times.[13] Sarsour subsequently released a statement acknowledging that "amidst this media storm [...] our values and our message have — too often — been lost [...] We regret that".[14] While this expression of regret did not end the controversy, it did at least reveal the fallibility of those who seek to act in the midst of bitter conflicts.

In August 2018, a video emerged of Jeremy Corbyn speaking in 2013 at a meeting of the Palestine Return Centre. In his speech he referred to the presence of some hostile Jewish Zionist observers at the meeting and quipped that they "don't understand English irony", despite having lived in the UK "for a very long time, probably all their lives".[15] While Corbyn has been repeatedly accused of tolerating antisemitism and backing antisemitic policies, this was a unique example of him saying something that had direct antisemitic connotations. What was antisemitic was the inference that the people he was talking about were not fully English, a common and very old trope. While some of Corbyn's detractors saw this speech as precious conformation of the primal antisemitism that lurks deep within his soul, the context suggests a more mundane scenario: He was deeply annoyed by at least one British Jewish Zionist activist who has a long history of turning up at pro-Palestinian events, filming and asking awkward questions. Under pressure, Corbyn's anger got the better of him and he fell back onto smug antisemitic rhetoric to express that anger.

Anti-racism has to be strong enough to withstand even those moments when the other is an absolute pain in the arse. While Corbyn possesses a sufficient capacity for civility even to Zionist Jews, it is apparently not sufficiently robust to carry him through times of anger. That is a very human failing, but of course not all humans proclaim their anti-racism at every opportunity and aspire to be leaders of diverse nations.

Not all anger stems from the tendency of human beings to simply be annoying. Anger can be righteous, sparked by horror at suffering, injustice and oppression. There is no question that much pro-Palestinian activity is motivated by this kind of anger (although this doesn't necessarily explain the tendency from those who are not Palestinian themselves to treat the Palestinian cause as "the" cause). How is minimal civility to be maintained when faced with Jews who defend the agents of so much suffering? How is minimal civility to be maintained between Jews and Muslims outside Israel–Palestine when they confront supporters of those who, they claim, wish them dead? When, in short, do we abandon even minimal civility?

I have already stated that living with diversity needs to hurt, and so should civility. I have also already argued that those outside of Israel–Palestine need to work to avoid the conflict eating the entire world: the anger of Palestinians and Israelis that live in the region should not be co-opted by those who sympathise with them. But there is no avoiding the fact that, at least during upsurges in violence in Israel–Palestine, civility will be tested to the point that it becomes simply unbearable to pursue. Even then, it remains necessary to have some kind of "backstop" in place, some kind of ethics of hatred that will mean that the abandonment of civility does not mean the abandonment of anti-racism.

That backstop, that ethics, can be formed out of self-interest. Anger and hate is inevitable, but it is not necessarily useful. "Does this help my cause?" can be as good a mantra as "Is this racist?". Someone enraged by the deaths of Palestinians in Gaza may think that Zionist Jews deserve to experience a bit of this pain. They may think that, in such circumstances, a concern for the feelings of Zionist Jews is utterly irrelevant. But would this actually help the situation?

In fact, hard-headed self-interest suggests that racism and antisemitism are usually counter-productive, whatever the cause. When Palestinians and their supporters fall into the repetition of classically antisemitic tropes about world Jewish conspiracies and Jewish blood-lust, they weaken their fight. Speaking purely militarily, the tactics you use to fight an occupying power are very different to those you use to fight a devilish, hydra-headed global monster. And treating Zionism as such a beast only intensifies Diaspora Jewish support for Israel. Similarly, shrill rhetoric about Islamisation and "creeping shariah" makes it almost impossible to pinpoint where Islamist movements present a danger and should be opposed.

Where Is the Limit?

Where is the limit? Where is the point at which we move beyond civility and ethics? Where is the point at which there is only resistance left, a resistance that requires the utter destruction of the other?

As I showed in Chapter Two, the Nazis have become synonymous with the place beyond this limit. And yes, the Nazis in the Second World War had to be resisted and defeated. There could be no compromise with them. They had placed themselves beyond the point where any kind of coexistence could have possibly been ethical. Perhaps one of the reasons why the Nazis are invoked so incessantly today is because we yearn for an imagined world of simple conflicts, where none of the tortuous questions I have raised in this chapter apply. However tempting it may be to seek the warm embrace of the place beyond civility, this is a desire that we should think very carefully about before we yield to it.

Nazis do exist today. Real, self-defined ones. And we are unquestionably living in an era in which racist authoritarian movements are growing in confidence and size. In some places they are in government. They must be resisted. They must be stopped. Unfortunately, this still does not take us as far into that place beyond as we might like. Pragmatic questions still persist, however much we might like to simply give vent to our rage. Ethical questions cannot be eradicated now, any more than they could be during the Second World War. You might believe, as Stalin did, that the mass rape of German women was ethically permissible as a "reward" for the soldiers who toiled fighting fascism. Maybe you think that Ann Coulter or Katie Hopkins deserve to be raped. Alternatively, maybe you think, as most UK and US leaders did most of the time, that even when facing a bestial enemy, no one should be raped and prisoners should not be tortured or starved. Whatever stance you take on these questions, they are still questions; the disgust that racists provoke in you does not absolve you from asking them.

Even if Nazis — those of today or those of yesterday — do not take us as far beyond the limit as we think, there was at least one way in which they represent an easier challenge than some hateful groups do today. The Nazis came from the ranks of the majority population of Germany and sought to eliminate or subjugate minorities in their own country, together with the countries they conquered. Similarly, today's neo-Nazis and their authoritarian racist cousins are usually drawn from majority or dominant ethnic groups of their countries. But how do we relate to those hateful, fascistic groups that are drawn from minority populations? The Islamic State, which advocates for rape, slavery and genocide, are as evil as the Nazis and cannot be tolerated in any fashion. But what do we do about their small but significant number of supporters within minority Muslim populations in Western countries? Are the normal rules of anti-racism suspended in their case? Are they freely killable, torturable, abuseable?

The answer has to be "no". However unpleasant it may be, different rules must apply to majorities and to minorities. We have to find a way to balance the need for monitoring minority extremists with a continuing commitment to managing diversity. And it gets worse: in a globalised world of diasporas, the distinction between an enemy "over there" and a troublesome minority "over here" is usually blurred. The internment of Japanese citizens in the US during the Second World War is widely and rightly regarded as a horrible injustice. Today, we are living in a world full of such troublesome minorities that inconvenience any notion of unrestrained geopolitical conflict that will not cause collateral damage outside the regions in question.

And it sucks.

No wonder the struggle against apartheid is such a popular model for pro-Palestinian activism. However valid or invalid comparisons between Israel and apartheid South Africa might be, they speak of a yearning for a struggle that posed none of the tortuous diasporic issues that Israel–Palestine does. There was a white South African diaspora in the apartheid years, but few were defenders of the regime. Collateral damage to this diaspora was not an issue, allowing activism to proceed unimpeded.

So even if you believe that Israel is an apartheid state or a Nazi state, you still have obligations, you still have to think about what that means for the Jewish minority who lives alongside you. Because Nazis do not take you into a world of glorious (un)ethical freedom. Nothing does.

Making Politics Possible

I started this book by arguing that the entangled knot of politics and group identity imperils anti-racism and gives rise to selective anti/semitism and other anti/racisms. With this book drawing to a close, it should be clear by now that I am arguing that there is no way to disentangle the knot and allow politics and anti-racism to proceed simultaneously, one unimpeded by the other. I am suggesting, rather, that the only way to preserve both politics and anti-racism is to practice both in a restrained, calculating and even cynical manner.

I wish it were otherwise, I really do.

Perhaps though, I might offer some crumb of comfort, a sketchy roadmap for how the political could be not liberated (nothing can do that) but at least loosened from its entanglements...

To see something as political is to see it as contestable, as if it could be other than it is. That contestability is why it is often so tempting to view certain spheres of life as "beyond" politics. The feminist dictum that "the personal is political" seeks to open up the private sphere of everyday life to the possibility that it could be different. The great achievement of contemporary critical theory has been to demonstrate the subtle and not-so-subtle ways in which much of our existence is rendered "natural", unchangeable, incontestable. But it is not easy to "denaturalise" the worlds we live in; it opens one up to tremendous insecurity. And when it is minority communities, such as Jews, who are asked, often aggressively, to expose their foundational commitments to the full force of political contestation, this process is all the more difficult. Indeed, as we have seen, such attempts often backfire, leading Jews to hold their Zionism even closer.

This is where anti-racism and political activism can and should go together. A central component of anti-racist practice should be enabling minorities to develop the confidence to transform some of their tightly-held beliefs and commitments into political positions. The pot of gold at the end of the anti-racist rainbow is a situation in which minorities can bear criticism of their politics. That can only happen if they are given the freedom to choose their politics for themselves. There can be no "wrong" choices. True anti-racism therefore requires fighting for the right of Jews to be Zionists, for Muslims to be Islamists and so on. That is the only way that there is even the slightest chance that they will be able to see their political choices as political choices, their foundational beliefs as politically contestable.

This means turning political activism into a strange kind of joint enterprise with potential political opponents. This is politics as a kind of invitation: join me in politicking! Let us make space together for an ideological battle!

Of course, this is not a process that can ever be completely successful; it can only work to a modest extent. It could though, lead to some clarity as to how politics should be conducted when it comes up against anti-racist commitments. Whether it is those Jews who are committed to the settlement project, those Palestinians who are committed to a Jew-free Palestine, those Muslims who are committed to blasphemy laws, those African Christians who are opposed to homosexuality — *opposing them means supporting them*, encouraging them to see themselves as political beings as well as bearers of identities. And the best place to start is with the self, by recognising that your politics is not separate from yourself, and by struggling honestly to understand where you end and your politics begins.

This then is a political practice worthy of diverse societies where identities and politics are entangled: Restrained, pragmatic, self-critical, yes, but also striving towards a world in which we might, one day, have the strength to deliberate freely over our different visions of what it is to be human.

Let the Self-Flagellation Begin...

I can't quite believe that I have been reduced to dolefully disinterring the corpses of the antediluvian values of restraint and civility. Somehow, I have ended up shrinking my idealism into proposing a weak, sullen form of coexistence.

But as John Maynard Keynes apocryphally said, "When the facts change, I change my mind. What do you do, sir?" The "fact" I am responding to is that we are now in a place where the possibilities of living tolerably alongside each other are being eroded as we speak. In this context, it may be that we have to look again at practices and values that we thought had been rendered either irrelevant or possibly reactionary. "Radical" is always relative, and we might be heading into a world where radical politics looks very different to what some of us have become used to.

Believe me, this is not the place I wanted to arrive at when I first conceived the idea of writing this book. I am fully aware of the appalling problems that the approach I have outlined in this chapter raises. I am sure you could read the subtext as something like:

> *Those Zionist Jews are over-sensitive and can't be weaned off their support for an oppressive state. So be smart! It's fine to hate Zionist Jews. But for goodness sake don't let on that this is how you feel! Stay calm, however much they provoke you, and watch your language. We'll defeat them in the end, but we can only do that if we're smart.*

And, from the other side, I'm sure you could criticise my approach as follows:

> *This is not an argument against antisemitism so much as an argument against the expression of antisemitism. It is foolhardy to assume that antisemitic attitudes don't matter unless they are expressed. Whatever happened to anti-racist education, to consciousness-raising, to challenging one's own prejudices?*

Don't misunderstand me: I want more than minimal civility. I yearn for dialogue, reconciliation, connection, empathy and profound encounters with the other. I have worked on dialogue projects myself and I know how life-changing it can be when you open yourself up to experiencing the world as others experience it. Even if the beliefs and identities that different peoples hold may be incommensurable, a broad range of philosophical traditions argue that we are still under an ethical obligation not just to tolerate the other but to listen to them too. As Richard J. Bernstein has argued:

> The plurality of rival incommensurable traditions imposes a universal responsibility upon reflective participants in any vital tradition — a responsibility that should not be confused with an indifferent superficial tolerance where no effort is made to understand and engage with the incommensurable otherness of "the Other".[16]

This is an ethical ideal that has rarely been as difficult to achieve as it is today, in a world where online communication turns even the most minor difference into an incommensurable one. In this context, even the accomplishment of a minimal civility that refuses any further effort of understanding is itself a very difficult challenge. And at least minimal civility preserves the possibility of developing into something more profound in the future. If we want an ethics of dialogue in the future, we may need, for now, to fight for the miserable cynicism of minimal civility. Or at least we should do that in public. While in the private sphere we could explore the possibilities of deep engagement in the other, the public sphere might be the place of wariness.

In any case, I am not just concerned with restraining the hatred that emerges from incommensurable differences. Selective love is as much of a problem as selective hate. Restraining excessive forms of philosemitism is as urgent a task as restraining antisemitism. The kind of love that leads to idealising the other and projecting one's fantasies onto them has damaged Jews and Palestinians. While it is inevitable that people will be drawn to certain kinds of Jews, it is essential to restrain the tendency to turn this into idealised love.

You could also find another set of problems with my argument:

> *You seem to be saying that diverse societies are a collection of discrete and bounded groups. In fact, you seem to want to draw the boundaries round them even more firmly. You essentialise ethno-religious identity. You leave no room for change, for fluidity and hybridity.*

No, I am not an essentialist. How could I be? My training as a sociologist has imbued me with an appreciation of the instability of identity, its fuzzy and hybrid frontiers. Yet anti-essentialism remains a minority pursuit. We have to act in a world where ethno-religious groups see their identities in essentialist ways. My approach pragmatically recognises the need for a form of civility than can allow essentialists to live together too. In any case, anti-essentialists are often only selective anti-essentialists, deconstructing the identities of some groups and putting others on pedestals: those who demonstrate the constructedness of Israeli identity, rarely do the same for Palestinian identity, and vice versa.

I recognise that mine is not an inspiring or exciting vision of the politics of diversity. Yet under current conditions, it is virtually a utopian one. So deeply have we become enmeshed in a selective approach to humanity that breaking free of this selectivity constitutes a monumental task. If we can free ourselves of selective delusions, then maybe we can create the basis for an anti-racism that is truly worthy of the name.

CONCLUSION

Paradise Regained

ללכ דחפל אל -רקיעהו ,דואמ רצ רשג ולוכ םלועה לכ

"All the world is a very narrow bridge, and the most important thing is not to be afraid."
— attributed to Reb Nachman of Breslov (1772–1810)

One of the things we have learned from the current antisemitism controversy is how difficult it is to be politically engaged within diverse societies without lapsing into hateful, racist language. Perhaps, amidst the post-war flight from antisemitism, racism and colonialism, we were naive about how difficult it would be to live with diversity. But that difficulty is not a reason to abandon the struggle. Rather, it is a reason to deepen it, just without illusions.

To live alongside the other is to live on a knife-edge, to walk on a narrow bridge. We are all of us capable of falling, and most of us will at some point. Perhaps a common recognition of how hard all of this is might be a good first step towards breaking out of the antisemitism controversy, out of a degraded anti-racist pietism, and towards a new world of genuine coexistence.

***

There is, of course, an alternative approach that I haven't suggested in this book: one that would go a long way to solving the antisemitism controversy and similar controversies over racism.

If you have fallen into the zone of selective anti/semite or any other kind of selective anti/racism, you always have the option of embracing consensual, full-blown racism; to hate openly and stridently.

After all, straightforward consensus racism was a common option until recently. You don't have to support the killing of all Jews to be a consensus antisemite — mild but palpable distaste is good enough. You don't have to support the enslavement of all people of colour — simple disgust at blackness is sufficient. Wouldn't it be a relief to break the endless circle of accusation and denial? Certainly, there are growing numbers who are taking this path. The (often hypocritical) unspeakability of racism in Western societies is starting to give way as far-right groups take power and whittle down their denials of racism from the heartfelt to the barely believable. Why not join in the fun?

As Dave Rich argues, we are surrounded by "antisemitism without antisemites", and, indeed, racism without racism.[1] It's time to return antisemitism to the antisemites — after all, they do it so much better. Racism needs to be given back to those who can really enjoy it.

It's time to make a choice: Either embrace full-blown, unambiguous hatred for everyone in a particular group or get used to the existence of minorities as they actually are. Either hate all Jews everywhere, or learn to live with the disappointing realisation that the Jews you have are the Jews you are going to get. Accept that there will always be Jews who hold politics that are hateful to you and that finding a way to live alongside them is more important than cosying up to the Jews you like. In fact, accepting Jews means cultivating some distance from the Jews to whom you are drawn.

For those who don't want to be consensus racists or antisemites, there is now no alternative to abandoning selective anti/racism. It's time to embark on the arduous path towards a reckoning with what anti-racism and the acceptance of diversity really means. Just as the Jewish question has proved the undoing of fantasies of a universal anti-racism, so attending to the mind-bending issues raised by the antisemitism controversy might clear the way back to an anti-racism that can survive the inevitable hatefulness of real human beings.

***

We Jews also have a choice to make.

We have been feeding the growth of selective anti/semitism and, by extension, selective anti/racism, for far too long. We have been offering ourselves up to be the chosen Jews, the good Jews, and damning our brethren. In doing so, we have colluded in the breakdown of anti-racism into a series of choices regarding which minorities to defend. That doesn't benefit us or anyone else in either the short- or long-term.

We have to decide whether we really want to fight selective anti/semitism — all of it, rather than just the segments which we dislike. If we take that choice we will have to take a path just as painful as that to be taken by those who refuse to be antisemites. We will need to refuse philosemitic love and insist on our common unlovability. We will have to show solidarity with those Jews who we think are not worthy of bearing the name. We will have to treat our extraordinary diversity as something other than a shop window to the world to select the Jews they like. That will not be a pleasant process.

We will also have to play our part in modelling the restraint that will be necessary to damp down the flames of antisemitic expression. It may be preferable, if difficult, for Jews to restrain some of the anger they feel about antisemitism. It may be smarter in some cases for Jews to accuse people of being rude, abusive, cruel or unfair rather than being antisemitic (even when they are). Given that many people who spread antisemitism these days do not want to be antisemites, minimal civility might preserve the possibility of carefully encouraging changes in behaviour. Forcing ourselves to be civil is a bitter pill to swallow, but what matters is long-term success, not the short-term rewards of venting pain.

And it would also help for Jews to look to their own racism. If we have learned anything in the last few decades it is that being a victim is no guarantee of moral purity. Even while insisting on the right of Jews — and anyone else — to be as hateful as they wish to be while still living free of antisemitism, it would help not to feed the beast. The same rules that apply to pro-Palestinian campaigners also apply to pro-Israel campaigners: Even the most impeccably liberal supporters of two-state liberal Zionism can, during times of war, fall back on stereotypes of Palestinians/Arabs as uncivilised.

***

As I finish this book, summer has turned into winter. The atmosphere in my local park is less carefree than when I began, as the prospect of another year of work, school and bad weather looms.

My fellow park-goers and I still haven't collapsed into paranoia. We remain watchful though, perhaps waiting for the inevitable revelation of our mutual otherness that will grind this multicultural idyll to dust. We are aware of our potential difference, we keep something of ourselves back, yet we carry on together.

For now, we are minimally civil to each other. Let's keep it that way. Let's keep a wary distance until we have the strength to do the work that will allow us to truly cope with that which divides us. To do so will be arduous. It will not happen automatically.

For now though, this cultivated space of mutual ignorance, this common delusion that we can live together, may be the closest thing we have to an earthly paradise.

NOTES

Preface: Humans, Politics and Identities

1 In chapter one, I explain why I follow the practice of spelling the word as "antisemitism" rather than "anti-Semitism".

Introduction: Harmony Corruption

1 Mark Fisher, *Capitalist Realism: Is There No Alternative?* (Zer0 Books, 2009).

Chapter One: What on Earth is Going On?

1 I defined what I mean by strangeness more fully in my article "On the Strangeness of Contemporary Antisemitism," *openDemocracy*, April 13, 2015, https://www.opendemocracy.net/keith-kahnharris/on-strangeness-of-contemporary-antisemitism.

2 Shami Chakrabarti, "The Shami Chakrabarti Inquiry," June 30, 2016.

3 J-TV, 2017 Whitewashed: Anti-Semitism in the Labour Party [online video] Available at: https://www.youtube.com/watch?v=te684rBHzOA [Accessed 5 October 2018].

4 Jessica Elgot and Nadia Khomami, "Labour Antisemitism Scandal Blamed for Tory Win in Barnet", *The Guardian*, May 4, 2018, , https://www.theguardian.com/politics/2018/may/04/labour-antisemitism-scandal-blamed-for-tory-win-in-barnet.

5 "Experiences and Perceptions of Antisemitism: Second Survey on Discrimination and Hate Crime against Jews in the EU," European Union Agency for Fundamental Rights (FRA), 2018

6 Glenn Thrush and Maggie Haberman, "Trump Is Criticized for Not Calling Out White Supremacists", *The New York Times*, December 22, 2017, https://www.nytimes.com/2017/08/12/us/trump-charlottesville-protest-nationalist-riot.html.

7 Ben Schreckinger, "The Alt-Right Comes to Washington", *POLITICO*, accessed October 5, 2018, https://www.politico.com/magazine/story/2017/01/alt-right-trump-washington-dc-power-milo-214629.

8 Daniel J. Roth, "U.S. Jewish Groups Laud Trump's 'courageous' Embassy Movet", *Jerusalem Post*, May 15, 2018, https://www.jpost.com/Diaspora/US-Jewish-groups-laud-Trumps-courageous-embassy-move-556426.

9 David Henkin, "The Big Picture: Jews and Trump", *Public Books*, November 9, 2017, http://www.publicbooks.org/big-picture-jews-and-trump/.

10 Sam Kestenbaum, "CUNY Under the Anti-Semitism Microscope", *The Forward*, March 30, 2016, https://forward.com/news/longform/337350/cuny-under-the-anti-semitism-microscope/.

11 "Experiences and Perceptions of Antisemitism: Second Survey on Discrimination and Hate Crime against Jews in the EU," European Union Agency for Fundamental Rights (FRA), 2018.

12 L. Daniel Staetsky, "Are Jews Leaving Europe?" Institute for Jewish Policy Research, 2017, http://archive.jpr.org.uk/object-eur137.

13 Anshel Pfeffer, "With Orban and Soros, Hungary's Jews Trapped Between pro-Israel and Anti-Semitic Politics", *Haaretz*, July 18, 2018, https://www.haaretz.com/world-news/europe/.premium.MAGAZINE-hungary-s-jews-trapped-between-pro-israel-and-anti-semitic-politics-1.6289081.

14 Ben Welch, "Notorious Right Wing Commentator Katie Hopkins Attends Zionist Federation Dinner", *Jewish Chronicle*, March 12, 2018, https://www.thejc.com/news/uk-news/notorious-right-wing-commentator-katie-hopkins-attends-zionist-federation-dinner-1.460455.

15 Max Blumenthal, "Hagee: Pro-Israel, Anti-Semitic?", *The Nation*, May 23, 2008, https://www.cbsnews.com/news/hagee-pro-israel-anti-semitic/.

16 Isabel Kershner, "Iran Deal Denounced by Netanyahu as 'Historic Mistake,'" *The New York Times*, December 21, 2017, https://www.nytimes.com/2015/07/15/world/middleeast/iran-nuclear-deal-israel.html.

17 Robert S. Wistrich, *Antisemitism: The Longest Hatred*. Pantheon Books, 1991.

18 Marcus, Kenneth L. *The Definition of Anti-Semitism*. Oxford University Press, 2015: 6

19 David Nirenberg, *Anti-Judaism: The Western Tradition*. W. W. Norton, 2013. [ebook]

20 David Engel, "Away from a Definition of Antisemitism. An Essay in the Semantics of Historical Description," in *Rethinking European Jewish History*, ed. Jeremy Cohen and Moshe Rosman (Oxford: Littman Library of Jewish Civilizations, 2009), 30–53.

21 David Feldman, "Toward a History of the Term 'Anti-Semitism,'" *The American Historical Review* 123, no. 4 (October 1, 2018): 1139–50.

22 "Working Definition of Antisemitism," International Holocaust Remembrance Alliance, May 26, 2016, https://www.holocaustremembrance.com/working-definition-antisemitism.

23 A copy of the code is embedded in the following article: Lee Harpin, "Read Labour's New Definition of Antisemitism That Has Caused so Much Anger," *The Jewish Chronicle*, July 5, 2018, https://www.thejc.com/comment/analysis/jeremy-corbyn-labour-definition-antisemitism-1.466626.

24 Ibid.

25 "Letter: As BAME Communities, We Stand United against Attempts to Suppress Our Voices," *The Independent*, August 17, 2018, https://www.independent.co.uk/voices/letters/letters-ihra-definition-palestine-israel-bame-sexism-labour-denmark-a8496251.html.

26 International Holocaust Remembrance Alliance 2016, *op. cit.*

27 For example: Brendan McGeever and David Feldman, "Corbyn's Labour, British Jews and Anti-Semitism: Will Peace Now Break Out?," *Haaretz*, September 6, 2018, https://www.haaretz.com/opinion/corbyn-s-labour-jews-and-anti-semitism-will-peace-now-break-out-1.6451772.

28 Antony Lerman, "Labour Should Ditch the IHRA Working Definition of Antisemitism Altogether," *openDemocracy*, September 4, 2018, https://www.opendemocracy.net/uk/antony-lerman/labour-should-ditch-ihra-working-definition-of-antisemitism-altogether.

29 Garfinkel, Harold. *Ethnomethodology's Program: Working Out Durkeim's Aphorism*. Rowman & Littlefield, 2002: 133-4

30 Daniel Staetsky. "Antisemitism in Contemporary Great Britain: Key Findings from the JPR Survey of Attitudes towards Jews and Israel." Institute for Jewish Policy Research, 2017. http://jpr.org.uk/publication?id=9993.

31 Rob Water, "Former Democratic Congresswoman, Cynthia McKinney, Flirts with Holocaust Deniers," *Intelligence Report*, November 30, 2009, https://www.splcenter.org/fighting-hate/intelligence-report/2009/former-democratic-congresswoman-cynthia-mckinney-flirts-holocaust-deniers.

32 Alice Walker, "It Is Our (Frightful) Duty To Study The Talmud", Alice Walker Official Website, 2017, http://alicewalkersgarden.com/2017/11/it-is-our-frightful-duty-to-study-the-talmud/

33 Joan Nathan, "Citizens Must Know If Their Political Candidates Hold Hateful Views," Tablet Magazine, November 2, 2018, https://www.tabletmag.com/jewish-news-and-politics/274161/voter-education.

Chapter Two: How Antisemitism and Racism Became Unspeakable

1 Garfield, Simon. *Our Hidden Lives: The Remarkable Diaries of Post-War Britain*. Random House, 2005.

2 Ibid. 132

3 Ibid. 244

4 Ibid. 257

5 Ibid. 509

6 Julius, Anthony. *Trials of the Diaspora: A History of Anti-Semitism in England*. Oxford University Press, 2010.

7 Kahn-Harris, Keith. *Denial. The Unspeakable Truth*. Notting Hill Editions, 2018.

8 Dr Aidan McGarry, *Romaphobia: The Last Acceptable Form of Racism*. Zed Books, 2017.

9 Bonilla-Silva, Eduardo. *Racism without Racists: Color-Blind Racism and the Persistence of Racial Inequality in America*. Rowman & Littlefield, 2013.

10 Mills, Charles. "White Ignorance." In *Race and Epistemologies of Ignorance*, edited by Shannon Sullivan and Nancy Tuana, 11–38. State University of New York Press, 2007.

11 See for example: Simon Harris, "Racism, Racialism and Race Realism: Taboo Words and the Power of Political Correctness," *European Defence League*, February 14, 2018, https://www.europeandefenceleague.com/2018/02/14/racism-racialism-and-race-realism-taboo-words-and-the-power-of-political-correctness/.

12 Robert Culkin, "Who Are The Proud Boys?," *Proud Boy Magazine*, August 24, 2017, http://officialproudboys.com/proud-boys/whoaretheproudboys/.

13 Rob Beschizza, "Is This the Ultimate 'I'm Not Racist, But…,'" *Boing Boing*, January 28, 2017, https://boingboing.net/2017/01/28/is-this-the-ultimate-im-no.html.

14 Marcus, Kenneth L. *The Definition of Anti-Semitism*. Oxford University Press, 2015: 11

15 Ibid. 14

16 Daniella Peled, "Dignity, Not Division, Should Be Jewish Response to Insignificant London Skinhead

Rally," *Haaretz*, June 29, 2015, https://www.haaretz.com/opinion/.premium-jews-must-respond-to-london-skinhead-rally-with-dignity-1.5374504.

17 Stone, Dan. "Genocide as Transgression." *European Journal of Social Theory* 7, no. 1 (2004): 45–65.

18 Sereny, Gitta. *Into That Darkness: From Mercy Killing to Mass Murder*. Random House, 1995: 200

19 Confino, Alon. *A World Without Jews: The Nazi Imagination from Persecution to Genocide*. Yale University Press, 2014: 14

20 Terrence McCoy, "Anti-Semitic Riots in Europe 'Took Us Back to 1938,'" *Washington Post*, July 23, 2014, https://www.washingtonpost.com/news/morning-mix/wp/2014/07/23/anti-semitic-riots-in-europe-took-us-back-to-1938/.

21 Jeffrey Goldberg, "Is It Time for the Jews to Leave Europe?," *The Atlantic*, April 2015, https://www.theatlantic.com/magazine/archive/2015/04/is-it-time-for-the-jews-to-leave-europe/386279/.

22 James Fallows, "The Central Question: Is It 1938?," *The Atlantic*, March 3, 2015, https://www.theatlantic.com/international/archive/2015/03/the-central-question-is-it-1938/386716/.

23 Tim Skirvin, "How to Post about Nazis and Get Away with It — the Godwin's Law FAQ," *Al.Usenet.Legends*, October 11, 1999, https://web.archive.org/web/19991011095714/http://www.faqs.org/faqs/usenet/legends/godwin/.

24 Leo Strauss, *Natural Right and History*, University of Chicago Press, 1965: 42-43

25 Rosenfeld, Gavriel D. *Hi Hitler!* Cambridge University Press, 2015.

26 Boswell, Matthew. *Holocaust Impiety in Literature, Popular Music and Film*. 2012 edition. Palgrave Macmillan, 2011: 3

27 For example: James Ball, "Stop Talking about Godwin's Law: Real Nazis Are Back," *New Statesman*, June 19, 2018, https://www.newstatesman.com/world/north-america/2018/06/stop-talking-about-godwin-s-law-real-nazis-are-back.

28 Godwin, Mike. Twitter Post. August 14, 2017, 1.03am. https://mobile.twitter.com/sfmnemonic/status/896884949634232320

Chapter Three: How The Jews Ruined Antisemitism

1 Jon Stone, "A Full Transcript of What Ken Livingstone Said about Antisemitism, Israel, Labour, and Naz Shah," *The Independent*, April 28, 2016, http://www.independent.co.uk/news/uk/politics/labour-anti-semitism-row-full-transcript-of-ken-livingstones-interviews-a7005311.html.

2 Brenner, Lenni. *Zionism in the Age of the Dictators*. On Our Own Authority! Publishing, 2014.

3 Paul Bognador, "Ken Livingstone's Claims Are an Insult to the Truth," *The Jewish Chronicle*, March 31, 2017, https://www.thejc.com/comment/comment/ken-livingstone-s-claims-are-an-insult-to-the-truth-1.435425.

4 See the document quoted in the following: Vaughan, James. Twitter Post. April 4, 2017, 1.21pm. https://twitter.com/EquusontheBuses/status/849235354158850050

5 For example: "Hitler, Insists Ken Livingstone," *NewsThump*, September 7, 2016, http://newsthump.com/2016/09/07/hitler-insists-ken-livingstone/.

6 Segev, Tom. *The Seventh Million: The Israelis and the Holocaust.* Translated by Haim Watzman. New York: Owl Books, 1991.

7 "Netanyahu: Hitler Didn't Want to Exterminate the Jews," *Haaretz,* October 21, 2015, https://www.haaretz.com/israel-news/netanyahu-absolves-hitler-of-guilt-1.5411578.

8 Arendt, Hannah. *Eichmann in Jerusalem: A Report on the Banality of Evil.* Penguin, 2006.

9 David Friedman, "Read Peter Beinart and You'll Vote Donald Trump," *Israel National News,* June 5, 2016, http://www.israelnationalnews.com/Articles/Article.aspx/18828.

10 Eli Valley, "Kapo, Kapow," *Jewish Currents,* June 27, 2018, https://jewishcurrents.org/comic/kapo-kapow.

11 Young, Isaac F, and Daniel Sullivan. "Competitive Victimhood: A Review of the Theoretical and Empirical Literature." *Current Opinion in Psychology,* Intergroup relations, 11 (October 1, 2016): 30–34.

12 Wendy Brown, "Wounded Attachments," *Political Theory* 21, no. 3 (1993): 390–410.

13 David Rieff, *In Praise of Forgetting: Historical Memory and Its Ironies.* Yale University Press, 2016.

14 Gabriel Noah Brahm Jr., "Holocaust Envy: The Libidinal Economy of the New Antisemitism.," *Journal for the Study of Antisemitism,* 2011, https://bit.ly/2sChtDp

15 For example: Roland Imhoff and Rainer Banse, "Ongoing Victim Suffering Increases Prejudice: The Case of Secondary Anti-Semitism," *Psychological Science* 20, no. 12 (December 1, 2009): 1443–47.

16 Dovid Katz, "On Three Definitions: Genocide, Holocaust Denial, Holocaust Obfuscation," in *A Litmus Test Case of*

Modernity: Examining Modern Sensibilities and the Public Domain in the Baltic States at the Turn of the Century (Peter Lang Publishers, 2009), 259–277.

17 Dovid Katz, "Is Eastern European 'Double Genocide' Revisionism Reaching Museums?," *Dapim: Studies on the Holocaust* 30, no. 3 (September 1, 2016): 191–220.

18 Finkelstein, Norman G. *The Holocaust Industry: Reflections on the Exploitation of Jewish Suffering*. Verso, 2003. Novick, Peter. *The Holocaust and Collective Memory*. London: Bloomsbury Publishing, 1999.

19 "A Portrait of Jewish Americans," Pew Research Center, October 1, 2013.

20 David Graham, Marlena Schmool, and Stanley Waterman, "Jews in Britain: A Snapshot from the 2001 Census", Institute for Jewish Policy Research, 2007.

21 "DC6207EW (NS-SeC by Religion by Sex by Age)," *Nomis — Official Labour Market Statistic*s, 2011, https://www.nomisweb.co.uk/census/2011/dc6207ew.

22 Jonathan Boyd, "Child Poverty and Deprivation in the British Jewish Community". Institute for Jewish Policy Research, March 31, 2011.

23 "A Portrait of Jewish Americans," Pew Research Center, October 1, 2013: 82.

24 Stephen Miller, Margaret Harris, and Colin Shindler, "The Attitudes of British Jews Towards Israel" (London: Department of Sociology School of Arts and Social Sciences City University London, 2015).

25 Keith Kahn-Harris, *Uncivil War: The Israel Conflict in the Jewish Community* (David/Paul, 2016); Dov Waxman, *Trouble in the Tribe: The American Jewish Conflict over Israel* (Princeton University Press, 2014).

26 "A Portrait of Jewish Americans," Pew Research Center, October 1, 2013: 82.

27 See for example: Steven M. Cohen and Ari Y. Kelman, eds., "Special Issue: Are Israel and Young American Jews Growing Apart: Debating the Distancing Hypothesis," *Contemporary Jewry* 30, no. 2–3 (2010): 141–319.

28 Peter Beinart, "The Failure of the American Jewish Establishment," *New York Review of Books*, May 12, 2010, http://www.nybooks.com/articles/archives/2010/jun/10/failure-american-jewish-establishment/?pagination=false.

29 D. Waxman, "The Israel Lobbies: A Survey of the Pro-Israel Community in the United States," *Israel Studies Forum* 25, no. 1 (2010): 5–28.

30 Michael Alexander, *Jazz Age Jews*, Princeton University Press, 2001.

31 Howard Jacobson has often satirised this "you of all people" trope. See, for example: Howard Jacobson, "Ludicrous, Brainwashed Prejudice," *The Independent*, April 23, 2011, http://www.independent.co.uk/voices/commentators/howard-jacobson/howard-jacobson-ludicrous-brainwashed-prejudice-2273774.html.

32 See for example: Steve Cohen, *That's Funny, You Don't Look Antisemitic: Antiracist Analysis of Left Antisemitism*. Beyond the Pale Collective, 1984; Robert Fine and Philip Spencer, *Antisemitism and the Left: On the Return of the Jewish Question*. Manchester University Press, 2017.

33 Dave Rich, *The Left's Jewish Problem: Jeremy Corbyn, Israel and Anti-Semitism/* Biteback Publishing, 2016; David Hirsh, *Contemporary Left Antisemitism*. Routledge, 2017.

34 April Rosenblum, "The Past Didn't Go Anywhere:

Making Resistance to Antisemitism Part of All Our Movements," 2007. Archived at: https://archive.org/details/ThePastDidntGoAnywhere: 1

35 Bouteldja, Houria. *Whites, Jews, and Us: Toward a Politics of Revolutionary Love*. Semiotexte/Smart Art, 2017: 64

36 Jacqueline Rose, *The Question of Zion*. Princeton University Press, 2007.

37 Brian Klug, "Two Faces of Zionism," Building The Bridge, November 14, 2018, https://buildingthebridge.eu/common-ground/general/two-faces-of-zionism/341.

38 Dave Rich, *The Left's Jewish Problem: Jeremy Corbyn, Israel and Anti-Semitism*, Biteback Publishing, 2016: 159-194

39 Joel Schalit, *Israel vs Utopia*. Akashic Books, 2009. 20, 34.

40 Frantz Fanon, *Black Skin, White Masks*. Pluto Press, 2008.

41 Michael Walzer, *Exodus and Revolution*. Basic Books, 1985.

42 "The Trump administration has not hidden its frustration that his pro-Israel steps — highlighted by the embassy move — have not been met with appropriate recognition and gratitude from many American Jews": *The Jewish State at 70*. Jewish People Policy Institute, 2018: 56.

43 Nathan Guttman, "Out of Blue, Midwest Vote Becomes Israel Scrap," *The Forward*, July 13, 2012, https://forward.com/news/israel/159239/out-of-blue-midwest-vote-becomes-israel-scrap/; Debra Nussbaum Cohen, "At Summit to Counter BDS Movement, J Street Feels the Heat," *Haaretz*, March 31, 2017, https://www.haaretz.com/us-news/.premium-at-summit-to-counter-bds-movement-j-street-feels-the-heat-1.5455370.

44 Natasha Mozgovaya, "Glenn Beck, George Soros and a Row About the Holocaust," *Haaretz*, November 12, 2010, https://www.haaretz.com/1.5138791.

Chapter Four: The Chosen Ones

1 Keith Kahn-Harris, "Searching for the Real Jews," *Boundless*, May 8, 2018, https://unbound.com/boundless/2018/05/09/searching-for-the-real-jews/.

2 Agence France-Presse, "AfD Provokes Outcry in Germany with Launch of 'Jewish Group,'" *The Guardian*, October 7, 2018, https://www.theguardian.com/world/2018/oct/07/germanys-afd-sparks-outcry-with-launch-of-jewish-group.

3 Ben Sales, "Naftali Bennett: Blaming Trump for Pittsburgh Shooting Is 'Unfair,'" Jewish Telegraphic Agency, October 30, 2018, https://www.jta.org/2018/10/30/news-opinion/united-states/naftali-bennett-blaming-trump-pittsburgh-shooting-unfair.

4 "Himmler's 10/04/43 Posen Speech," The Nizkor Project, accessed November 3, 2017, http://www.nizkor.org/hweb/people/h/himmler-heinrich/posen/oct-04-43/.

5 Adam Hochschild, *King Leopold's Ghost: A Story of Greed, Terror and Heroism in Colonial Africa*. London: Pan Books, 2002.

6 Brodkin, Karen. *How Jews Became White Folks and What That Says About Race in America*. New Brunswick, NJ.: Rutgers University Press, 1998.

7 Yuval-Davis, Nira, Georgie Wemyss, and Kathryn Cassidy. "Everyday Bordering, Belonging and the Reorientation of British Immigration Legislation." *Sociology* 52, no. 2 (April 1, 2018): 228–44.

8 "Britain First and 'Racism' — The Truth!," Britain First, accessed September 20, 2018, https://www.britainfirst.org/racism.

9 Jakobovits, Immanuel. "From Doom to Hope: A Jewish View on 'Faith in the City', the Report of the Archbishop of Canterbury's Commission on Urban Priority Areas." Office of the Chief Rabbi, January 1986: 7

10 Esther Romeyn, "Anti-Semitism and Islamophobia: Spectropolitics and Immigration," *Theory, Culture & Society* 31, no. 6 (November 1, 2014): 77–101,

11 At a late stage in preparing this book, I discovered a paper that also describes "selective philosemitism" in its discussion of the Dutch anti-Muslim politician Geert Wilders: Evelien Gans, "Anti-Antisemitic Enthusiasm & Selective Philosemitism: Geert Wilders, the PVV and the Jews" (Antisemitism in Europe Today: the Phenomena, the Conflicts, Berlin: Jewish Museum Berlin, 2013), https://www.jmberlin.de/sites/default/files/antisemitism-in-europe-today_6-gans.pdf.

12 Kate DeMolder, "Ian Paisley Jr Apologises for Sharing Racially Inappropriate Tweet," *JOE.ie*, accessed October 11, 2018, https://www.joe.ie/news/ian-paisley-jr-apologise-tweet-621178.

13 "Theresa May: It 'sickens' Me That Nearly 40 per Cent of Jews Would Consider Emigrating If Corbyn Got In," The Jewish Chronicle, September 17, 2018, https://www.thejc.com/news/uk-news/theresa-may-jc-poll-suggesting-40-per-cent-of-british-jews-would-consider-emigrating-sickens-me-1.469941.

14 Burchill, Julie. *Unchosen*. Unbound, 2014.

15 Emily Dugan, "What Did This Lesbian Rabbi Do to Make Julie Burchill Mad?," *The Independent*, September 26, 2014, http://www.independent.co.uk/news/

people/what-did-this-lesbian-rabbi-do-to-make-julie-burchill-mad-9758896.html.

16 Zygmunt Bauman, "Allosemitism: Premodern, Modern, Postmodern," ed. Bryan Cheyette and Laura Marcus, *Modernity, Culture and 'the Jew*, 1998, 143–156: 143

17 Ibid. 146

18 Brossat, Alain, and Sylvie Klingberg. *Revolutionary Yiddishland: A History of Jewish Radicalism*. Verso, 2017.

19 Andrew Pierce, "They Raised a Beetroot in the Air and Shouted F*** Capitalism," *Mail Online*, April 3, 2018, http://www.dailymail.co.uk/news/article-5575579/They-raised-beetroot-air-shouted-f-capitalism.html.

20 Norman Podhoretz, "My Negro Problem--And Ours," *Commentary*, February 1, 1963, https://www.commentarymagazine.com/articles/my-negro-problem-and-ours/.

21 Adam Serwer, "Why Tamika Mallory Won't Condemn Farrakhan," The Atlantic, March 11, 2018, https://www.theatlantic.com/politics/archive/2018/03/nation-of-islam/555332/.

22 See, for example: Johannes Due Enstad, "Antisemitic Violence in Europe, 2005-2015 Exposure and Perpetrators in France, UK, Germany, Sweden, Norway, Denmark and Russia," HL Senteret: Senter for studier av Holocaust og livssynsminoriteter, 2017.

23 Scholars vary in their opinions on the relationship between Muslim and Christian antisemitism. For a useful introduction to this issue see: Martin Kramer, *The Salience of Islamic Antisemitism*, Institute of Jewish Affairs Report, no. 2, October 1995 http://martinkramer.org/sandbox/reader/archives/

the-salience-of-islamic-antisemitism/.See also: Bernard Lewis, *The Jews of Islam*. Princeton University Press, 1984; Walter Laqueur, Walter, *The Changing Face of Antisemitism: From Ancient Times To The Present Day*, Oxford University Press, 2006

24 James Renton and Ben Gidley, eds., *Antisemitism and Islamophobia in Europe: A Shared Story?* 2017: Palgrave Macmillan: 5

25 Ibid.

26 Uriya Shavit, "'Muslims Are the New Jews' in the West: Reflections on Contemporary Parallelisms," *Journal of Muslim Minority Affairs* 36, no. 1 (January 2, 2016): 1–15

27 Anya Topolski, "Good Jew, Bad Jew ... Good Muslim, Bad Muslim: 'Managing' Europe's Others," *Ethnic and Racial Studies* 41, no. 12 (September 26, 2018): 2179–96.

28 Bryan Cheyette, "Against Supersessionist Thinking: Old and New, Jews and Postcolonialism, the Ghetto and Diaspora," *Cambridge Journal of Postcolonial Literary Inquiry* 4, no. 3 (September 2017): 424–39.

29 *The Word*, Issue 26, April 2018

30 Patricia Hill Collins, *Black Feminist Thought: Knowledge, Consciousness and the Politics of Empowerment* Routledge, 1991; Kimberlé Crenshaw, "Demarginalizing the Intersection of Race and Sex: A Black Feminist Critique or Antidiscrimination Doctrine, Feminist Theory and Antiracist Politics," University of Chicago Legal Forum 1, (1989)

31 Ange-Maries Hancock, *Solidarity Politics for Millennials: A Guide to Ending the Oppression Olympics*. Springer, 2011: 18-19

32 Batya Ungar-Sargon, "Opinion | Intersectionality Has Abandoned Jews. Should We Abandon Intersectionality?," The Forward, May 15, 2018, https://forward.com/opinion/401007/intersectionality-has-abandoned-jews-should-we-abandon-intersectionality/.

33 Judith Butler, *Frames of War: When Is Life Grievable?* Verso, 2016.

34 "Judith Butler Responds to Attack: 'I Affirm a Judaism That Is Not Associated with State Violence,'" *Mondoweiss*, August 27, 2012, https://mondoweiss.net/2012/08/judith-butler-responds-to-attack-i-affirm-a-judaism-that-is-not-associated-with-state-violence/.

35 Rohini Hensman, *Indefensible: Democracy, Counterrevolution, and the Rhetoric of Anti-Imperialism*, Haymarket Books, 2018.

36 See, for example: Collier Meyerson, "Can You Be a Zionist Feminist? Linda Sarsour Says No," *The Nation*, March 13, 2017, https://www.thenation.com/article/can-you-be-a-zionist-feminist-linda-sarsour-says-no/; Steven Salaita, "Zionists Should Be Excluded from Left-Oriented Protests," *Mondoweiss*, January 30, 2018, https://mondoweiss.net/2018/01/zionists-excluded-oriented/.

37 4G Live TV, 2018 *Jenny Manson (Co-Chair of JVL) speaking at Palestinian Women Speak Out, LMC, 19th March 2018* [online video] Available at: https://www.youtube.com/watch?v=OxULZKEhN4g URL [Accessed 5 October 2018].

38 David J. Wertheim, ed., *The Jew as Legitimation: Jewish-Gentile Relations Beyond Antisemitism and Philosemitism*. Springer, 2017.

39 For example: "Lincoln's Blood Libel and Seven Jewish Children," Community Security Trust, January 20, 2011, https://cst.org.uk/news/blog/2011/01/20/lincolns-blood-libel-and-seven-jewish-children. The full text of the play can be found here: "Read Caryl Churchill's Seven Jewish Children," *The Guardian*, February 26, 2009, sec. Stage, https://www.theguardian.com/stage/2009/feb/26/caryl-churchill-seven-jewish-children-play-gaza.

40 Mahmood Mamdani, "Good Muslim, Bad Muslim: A Political Perspective on Culture and Terrorism," *American Anthropologist* 104, no. 3 (2002): 766–75.

41 Ayaan Hirsi Ali, *Heretic: Why Islam Needs a Reformation Now*. New York, Harper, 2015.

42 "Why Stop the War Don't Want to Listen to Syrians," Left Foot Forward, November 12, 2015, https://leftfootforward.org/2015/11/why-stop-the-war-dont-want-to-listen-to-syrians/.

43 Olivia Solon, "How Syria's White Helmets Became Victims of an Online Propaganda Machine," *The Guardian*, December 18, 2017, https://www.theguardian.com/world/2017/dec/18/syria-white-helmets-conspiracy-theories.\

Chapter Five: Whom Should We Listen to Now?

1 David Hirsh, *Contemporary Left Antisemitism*, Routledge, 2017: 11

2 Linda Sarsour, "A Letter on Loyalty, Agency, Unity and the Farrakhan Controversy," November 18, 2018, https://mavenroundtable.io/lindasarsour/politics/a-letter-on-loyalty-agency-unity-and-the-farrakhan-controversy-EqyktSghwkywYL1jKsADdQ/.

3 Jewish Voice for Peace, *On Antisemitism: Solidarity and the Struggle for Justice*. Haymarket Books, 2017: 18

4 Jean-Paul Sartre, *Anti-Semite and Jew: An Exploration of the Etiology of Hate*, New York: Schocken Books, 1976: 6

5 Ibid. 13

6 William MacPherson, "The Stephen Lawrence Inquiry" (London, February 1999): Recommendation 12

7 Jessica Elgot, "Labour Antisemitism Code Could Breach Equality Act," *The Guardian*, July 16, 2018, https://www.theguardian.com/politics/2018/jul/16/labour-antisemitism-code-could-breach-equality-act. For a contrary view, see: David Pavett, "Racism/Antisemitism: What 'MacPherson Principle'?," Jewish Voice for Labour, July 15, 2018, https://www.jewishvoiceforlabour.org.uk/blog/the-macpherson-principle/.

8 Etan, Haya. Twitter Post. 8 January 2016, 6.00am. https://twitter.com/TeachESL/status/685340218908631040

9 Jonathan Boyd and Daniel Staetsky, "Could It Happen Here? What Existing Data Tell Us about Contemporary Antisemitism in the UK". London: Institute for Jewish Policy Research, 2015.

10 Jimmy Carter, *Palestine Peace Not Apartheid*, Simon and Schuster, 2007. For one of the more measured, yet still strong, criticisms, see: Deborah Lipstadt, "Jimmy Carter's Jewish Problem," *Washington Post*, January 20, 2007, http://www.washingtonpost.com/wp-dyn/content/article/2007/01/19/AR2007011901541.html.

11 Jamie Hakim, "Affect and Popular Zionism in the British Jewish Community after 1967," *European Journal of Cultural Studies* 18, no. 6 (December 2015): 672–89;

Ilan Zvi Baron, *Obligation in Exile: The Jewish Diaspora, Israel and Critique*, Edinburgh University Press, 2015.

12 Justin Jalil and Raphael Ahren, "Netanyahu to French Jews: 'Israel Is Your Home,'" *Times of Israel*, January 10, 2015, http://www.timesofisrael.com/netanyahu-to-french-jews-israel-is-your-home/.

13 "Hamas Covenant 1988," The Avalon Project, accessed September 27, 2018, http://avalon.law.yale.edu/20th_century/hamas.asp.

14 For example: Victor Sharpe, "The Counterfeit Arabs," *Israel National News*, November 20, 2013, http://www.israelnationalnews.com/Articles/Article.aspx/14126.

15 Josh Nathan-Kazis and Nikki Casey, "A New Wave Of Hardline Anti-BDS Tactics Are Targeting Students, And No One Knows Who's Behind It," *The Forward*, accessed October 9, 2018, https://forward.com/news/national/407127/a-new-wave-of-hardline-anti-bds-tactics-are-targeting-students-and-no-one/.

16 For example: Anne Karpf et al., eds., *A Time to Speak Out: Independent Jewish Voices on Israel, Zionism and Jewish Identity* (London: Verso, 2008); David Landy, *Jewish Identity and Palestinian Rights: Diaspora Jewish Opposition to Israel* (London: Zed Books, 2011); Ben Welch, "Young Zionists 'will Not Bow to Intimidation' after Gaza Kaddish Participants Abused," *The Jewish Chronicle*, July 6, 2018, https://www.thejc.com/news/uk-news/gaza-kaddish-israel-tour-reform-judaism-nina-morris-evans-1.466765.

17 Dave Rich, *The Left's Jewish Problem: Jeremy Corbyn, Israel and Anti-Semitism*, Biteback Publishing, 2016: 122

18 Leora Batnitzky, *How Judaism Became a Religion: An Introduction to Modern Jewish Thought* (Princeton, NJ: Princeton University Press, 2013).
19 Kwame Anthony Appiah, *The Lies That Bind: Rethinking Identity*. Profile Books, 2018: 217-218
20 Michael Tracey, "Anti-Semitism Is Horrible, But Not A Dominant Force In American Life," *TYT Network*, February 22, 2017, https://medium.com/theyoungturks/anti-semitism-is-horrible-but-not-a-dominant-force-in-american-life-e7d008e0fc37.
21 Alexander Cockburn, "My Life as an 'Anti-Semite,'" *Counterpunch Newsletter*, September 1, 2003. Archived at: http://student.cs.ucc.ie/cs1064/jabowen/IPSC/articles/article0004256.html.
22 Melanie Kaye/Kantrowitz, *The Colors of Jews: Racial Politics and Radical Diasporism*. Indiana University Press, 2007.
23 For more on Israeli collusion in denial of the Armenia genocide, see: Yair Auron, *The Banality of Denial: Israel and the Armenian Genocide*, New Brunswick: Transaction Publishers, 2003.
24 John Elder, "Rising anti-semitism cannot be tackled without addressing Israel's crimes", *The Morning Star*, June 18, 2018. https://morningstaronline.co.uk/article/rising-anti-semitism-cannot-be-tackled-without-addressing-israel%E2%80%99s-crimes
25 Alain Badiou, Eric Hazan, and Ivan Segré, *Reflections on Anti-Semitism*. Verso Books, 2013: 14
26 Lenni Brenner "Anti-Semitism, Old and New" 39-41 in Cockburn, Alexander, and Jeffrey St Clair. The Politics of Anti-Semitism. AK Press, 2003: 41

27 Robert Cohen, "The Jewish Establishment's 'War Against Corbyn' Risks Bringing Real Antisemitism to Britain," *Writing from the Edge* , July 28, 2018, http://www.patheos.com/blogs/writingfromtheedge/2018/07/the-jewish-establishments-war-against-corbyn-risks-bringing-real-antisemitism-to-britain/.

28 Hannah Arendt, *Antisemitism: Part One of The Origins of Totalitarianism* Houghton Mifflin Harcourt, 2012.

Chapter Six: How to Cope with Diversity

1 For the information of non-UK readers, "todger" is British slang for penis.

2 I'm grateful to Caroline Bressey for suggesting this historical interpretation to me.

3 Gilroy, Paul. *After Empire: Melancholia Or Convivial Culture?* Routledge, 2004: 166

4 Les Back and Shamser Sinha, "Multicultural Conviviality in the Midst of Racism's Ruins," *Journal of Intercultural Studies* 37, no. 5 (September 2, 2016): 517–32.

5 Steven Vertovec, "Super-Diversity and Its Implications," *Ethnic and Racial Studies* 30, no. 6 (November 1, 2007): 1024–54.

6 Richard Sennett, *Together: The Rituals, Pleasures and Politics of Cooperation* Penguin, 2012.

7 Ibid. 246

8 Anthony Julius, *Trials of the Diaspora: A History of Anti-Semitism in England,* Oxford University Press, 2010: 6-11

9 Gavin I. Langmuir, *Toward a Definition of Antisemitism,* University of California Press, 1996.

10 Steven Salaita, *Uncivil Rites : Palestine and the Limits of Academic Freedom*. Haymarket, 2015: 42

11 Charles P. Pierce, "The Civility Debate Has Reached Peak Stupidity," Esquire, June 25, 2018, https://www.esquire.com/news-politics/politics/a21931194/sarah-huckabee-sanders-red-hen-civility/; Laurel Leff, "The Trump Civility Debate Isn't New. In the 1930s, America Debated Whether It Was Civil to Shun the Nazis," *Haaretz*, June 28, 2018, https://www.haaretz.com/us-news/.premium-america-s-fear-of-incivility-appeased-nazism-we-can-t-go-there-again-1.6220593.

12 Keith Kahn-Harris, *Uncivil War: The Israel Conflict in the Jewish Community*, David Paul, 2016.

13 For a nuanced, critical take on Sarsour's comments, see: Batya Ungar-Sargon, "The Women's March Is Abusing Its Power — By Pretending It Doesn't Exist," The Forward, November 19, 2018, https://forward.com/opinion/414470/the-womens-march-is-abusing-its-power-by-pretending-it-doesnt-exist/.

14 "Women's March Response to Recent Critiques", November 20 2018, https://drive.google.com/file/d/17CInucXjr6UHdFwXpJ-XvP-Qc08k9qMn/view?fbclid=IwAR2qZ_2VP2tpkyIeM-JCJOJHE4pYT4gfDgxbsTWrtvJb0T7lD-Q8l0h73Xc (Accessed 21 November 2018)

15 "Corbyn Defends 'British Zionist' Comments," *BBC News*, August 25, 2018, https://www.bbc.com/news/uk-politics-45301548.

16 Richard J. Bernstein, *The New Constellation: The Ethical-Political Horizons of Modernity / Postmodernity*. John Wiley & Sons, 2013: 66

Conclusion: Paradise Regained

1 Dave Rich, *The Left's Jewish Problem: Jeremy Corbyn, Israel and Anti-Semitism* Biteback Publishing, 2016: 250

ACKNOWLEDGEMENTS (SORT OF)

I'd like to write an acknowledgements section, I really would. But what would happen if I did?

Readers who are heavily invested in the antisemitism controversy, from whatever perspective, would scan the list of names, checking to see who I might be allied with. On that basis, readers might decide whether or not what they have read can be trusted, whether I am worth listening to. It matters not what I say, but to whom I have listened. The search for such "gotcha" moments can imperil the possibility that a book's arguments are seriously considered.

The truth is, I have learned from many people about antisemitism, racism, diversity and much else. This book was born out of conversations and encounters with a range of scholars, activists and regular folks. Were I to attempt to list them, it would not matter that the list is fairly diverse. The presence of one of the hateful ones would be enough to poison this whole book for some readers. And there is an opposite danger too: that acknowledging that I have learned from many different people would be seen as a sign of a pathetic attempt to be even-handed on an issue where there is no alternative but to choose sides.

Should it need to be said that learning from a wide range of people does not mean that I agree with them on everything?

Maybe, in today's febrile political environment, it is better not to acknowledge the fact of having learned from real human beings. To do so wouldn't just risk undermining my credentials with certain readers, it would also unfairly yoke those to whom I have listened to me and the arguments I make.

The only people I will risk mentioning are my family. They have given me the freedom to laugh at my absurdities and the absurdities of the issues in which I am invested. I had thought of dedicating this book to my children "in the hope that they grow up into a world where antisemitism does not exist". That they, and my wife too, would see this as sanctimonious bullshit is another reason why I owe them more than I can express.

Repeater Books

is dedicated to the creation of a new reality. The landscape of twenty-first-century arts and letters is faded and inert, riven by fashionable cynicism, egotistical self-reference and a nostalgia for the recent past. Repeater intends to add its voice to those movements that wish to enter history and assert control over its currents, gathering together scattered and isolated voices with those who have already called for an escape from Capitalist Realism. Our desire is to publish in every sphere and genre, combining vigorous dissent and a pragmatic willingness to succeed where messianic abstraction and quiescent co-option have stalled: abstention is not an option: we are alive and we don't agree.